praise for

what
JESUS
is all about

Dr. Henrietta Mears directly discipled hundreds of young people whom God led into full-time Christian ministry. Today, no doubt, the thousands of disciples they influenced are, in turn, introducing millions of people to Christ. Henrietta's life was one of spiritual multiplication, and the world is a better place in which to live because she surrendered her life as a young woman to the Lord Jesus Christ to serve Him with all her heart.

DR. WILLIAM R. BRIGHT
PRESIDENT, CAMPUS CRUSADE FOR CHRIST

I caught from Henrietta Mears, as from no other woman, the Christian life—not only from her teaching, but also from her living. On a daily basis God allowed her personal, vibrant, positive, practical and persuasive words and lifestyle to penetrate my life. She generously shared her life with Bill and me, and that caused us to love and appreciate her for what she truly was—a woman of God!

VONETTE BRIGHT
CAMPUS CRUSADE FOR CHRIST

One of the greatest Christians I have ever known.

BILLY GRAHAM

what
JESUS
IS aLL abOut

DR. HENRIETTA C. MEARS

Regal

From Gospel Light
Ventura, California, U.S.A.

PUBLISHED BY REGAL BOOKS
FROM GOSPEL LIGHT
VENTURA, CALIFORNIA, U.S.A.
PRINTED IN THE U.S.A.

Regal Books is a ministry of Gospel Light, a Christian publisher dedicated to serving the local church. We believe God's vision for Gospel Light is to provide church leaders with biblical, user-friendly materials that will help them evangelize, disciple and minister to children, youth and families.

It is our prayer that this Regal book will help you discover biblical truth for your own life and help you meet the needs of others. May God richly bless you.

For a free catalog of resources from Regal Books/Gospel Light, please call your Christian supplier or contact us at 1-800-4-GOSPEL *or* www.regalbooks.com.

Introduction and study guide written by Bayard Taylor • Edited by Amy Spence
Cover design by Robert Williams • Interior design by Stephen Hahn

Library of Congress Cataloging-in-Publication Data
Mears, Henrietta C. (Henrietta Cornelia), 1890–
  What Jesus is all about / Henrietta C. Mears.
    p. cm.
  ISBN 0-8307-3327-2
  1. Jesus Christ—Person and offices. 2. Bible. N.T.
Gospels—Criticism, interpretation, etc. I. Title.
  BT203.M43 2004
  232—dc22
                                                        2003024895

Rights for publishing this book in other languages are contracted by Gospel Light Worldwide, the international nonprofit ministry of Gospel Light. Gospel Light Worldwide also provides publishing and technical assistance to international publishers dedicated to producing Sunday School and Vacation Bible School curricula and books in the languages of the world. For additional information, visit www.gospellightworldwide.org; write to Gospel Light Worldwide, P.O. Box 3875, Ventura, CA 93006; or send an e-mail to info@gospellightworldwide.org.

taBle of contents

Introduction...7

Chapter 1...14
Understanding the Gospels
The Gospels Portray Jesus Christ, Our Savior and Lord

Chapter 2...32
Understanding Matthew
Matthew Portrays Jesus Christ, the Promised Messiah

Chapter 3...63
Understanding Mark
Mark Portrays Jesus Christ, the Servant of God

Chapter 4...96
Understanding Luke
Luke Portrays Jesus Christ, the Son of Man

Chapter 5...124
Understanding John
John Portrays Jesus Christ, the Son of God

Chapter 6...162
Understanding Acts
Acts Portrays Jesus Christ, the Living Lord

Introduction

Few people would disagree that Jesus of Nazareth is the most famous, most popular, most revered and most important person who has ever lived on this planet. For this reason alone, it makes sense to find out about who Jesus is and what He stands for.

For the most part, wherever we go, whenever people find out about Jesus—whether through the Bible, radio, literature or film—they are almost irresistibly attracted to Him. They want to find out more. They desire to have Jesus on their side. They want to appropriate Jesus in some way, to show how Jesus would fit with their most deeply held values. They instinctively recognize the goodness and truth of Jesus' teachings; and they appreciate that Jesus was in some way especially connected to what is ultimately real.

This is true across every cultural, ethnic and religious tradition. It doesn't matter what continent, tribe or clan people are from or whether they are Hindus, Buddhists, Muslims, Taoists, animists or Marxists! Although not every person is attracted to Jesus, the multitudes are.

Even Jewish people are taking another look at Jesus today. This is somewhat surprising, because Jewish people may very well have ample reasons to avoid the issue of Jesus due to the long history of Christian persecution of Jews in the West. Nevertheless, notable Jewish writers are recognizing a sympathetic figure in the Jesus of the first century. Jesus was a Jewish person, much like them, who revered the Scriptures, operated in the prophetic tradition and endured unjust persecution.

This new, positive attitude is something that was nearly unheard of only a generation or two ago.

A WORLD RELIGION

For hundreds of years, the knowledge of Jesus was pretty much confined to portions of the Middle East and the backwaters of Europe. Great civilizations in the East, Asia, Africa and the Americas rose and fell, oblivious to Jesus' person and message. Little beachheads of sold-out Jesus communities of faith were established in some of these areas, but the majority of people never had an opportunity to hear about Him.

In the past four hundred years, however, the picture has changed drastically. Both working with and against many factors (i.e., intellectual movements, science, explorative discoveries, development of trade routes, colonialism, slavery, wars, Christian missions, and so on), Christianity is the first religion to truly establish itself worldwide.

However, merely recognizing Christianity as a world religion doesn't answer the question, Why is Jesus almost universally popular? To answer that question, we need to examine the main source of Christian faith. If we want to know about Jesus, we will need to start with the Bible—in particular, the Gospels and the book of Acts.

THE GOSPELS

The Gospels—Matthew, Mark, Luke and John—are literature, but they are unique to all of world literature.

The Gospels are solidly grounded in actual historical

events, but they are not history in the modern sense of pin-pointing an exact sequence of events. They contain dialogues, but they are not merely give-and-take conversations that teach us precise thinking or a particular religious path. They contain speeches that move people both rationally and emotionally, but they do not focus on techniques of persuasion. They contain miracle stories, but they are not mythological. They teach morals, but they have nothing to do with giving us a moralistic rule book. They contain the greatest love story ever told, but they are not romance novels.

Then what *is* the intended purpose of the first four books of the New Testament? What *is* Jesus all about?

When we read the Gospels, we are not just reading about a dead guy who lived two thousand years ago who said and did a lot of nice things. The Gospels are intended to bring us face-to-face with the *living* person of Jesus Christ.

In other words, when Jesus heals the blind man, we are in the crowd, or we are the blind man who now sees. When Jesus walks on water, we are with the disciples on the boat, drenched by rowdy waves, scared witless and wondering what's going on. When Jesus says, "I am the bread of life" (John 6:35), we have to figure out what in the world He's talking about. When Jesus urges us, "Follow Me" (Matt. 4:19; Mark 1:17), we have a personal and existential choice to make—to allow the living Jesus into our lives, which brings spiritual birth into our hearts and transforms us by His presence, or to keep going our own way.

In short, in all of human literature, there is nothing that compares with the Gospels, because there is no one who rivals the living Jesus. He knows the human condition better than anyone else.

Who needs a role model? Who desires truth, beauty and goodness? Who has sorrow? Who needs forgiveness for selfish, wrong acts? Who needs healing—psychological, physical and spiritual? Who needs meaning in life, whether things are good or have gone dreadfully bad? Who needs unconditional love and a place to belong?

We do. We need to allow Jesus to meet us at our point of need. As we read the Gospels, let's allow Jesus do His work in our lives. It will be a good and beautiful work.

Remember, it's not always an easy road. We're going to have to put some sandals on and get dusty with Jesus on the rocky trails of Galilee; but as we do, we'll see how Jesus treats women, children, sick people and outcasts with the utmost respect and dignity. We'll be struck by His tenderness and surprised by His fierceness. We might even shout in shock or fear—or taste salty tears of joy—at His miracles. Let us entertain the possibility that maybe, just maybe, this same Jesus will meet us in the way He met people in the first century.

THE BOOK OF ACTS

Once we have read the Gospels, we'll explore the rollicking excitement of the book of Acts. The book of Acts will be our initiation into the adventure of what it means to be part of the worldwide Jesus movement. The book of Acts shows us how, after dying on the Cross, the same Jesus who had lived among His followers somehow continued to work in and with them. Just as Jesus took diverse and imperfect people under His wing then, so He continues today to mold His followers into a people—hearts aflame with love and dismissive of personal danger and cost—who are His representatives in a needy world. Will we associate ourselves with the greatest person who has ever lived? That is the ultimate question.

HENRIETTA MEARS

Henrietta Mears wrote *What the Bible Is All About,* which this book, *What Jesus Is All About,* is based on. Mears was one of the most remarkable Christian women of the twentieth century. Born in Minnesota in 1890, she came to California in 1928 to become the director of Christian education at Hollywood Presbyterian Church. She stayed at Hollywood Presbyterian until her death in 1963. During her ministry, she gained world-wide recognition and prominence.

Henrietta Mears was a multitalented, godly woman. Among other things, she taught the college class at Hollywood Presbyterian; oversaw the production of an entirely new Sunday School approach, which in turn led to the formation of Gospel Light Publications and Regal Books; influenced many of the twentieth century's greatest male Christian leaders through conferences and personal contacts; spearheaded the Forest Home Christian Camp; and founded Gospel Light Worldwide, a nonprofit organization dedicated to translating the best of Christian literature into foreign languages.

One of her most wonderful legacies is her book *What the Bible Is All About.* The book is a condensation of teachings she developed for high school students in the 1930s. It continues to sell tens of thousands of copies each year.

What Jesus Is All About introduces some of Henrietta Mears's teachings—those on Jesus—to a new generation of readers. It also includes study questions after each chapter. Throughout the book, you'll notice that selected scriptures are contained within shaded boxes. These Scripture passages are highlighted because they are either Old Testament prophecies fulfilled by Jesus or they are an Old Testament passage(s) describing a promise and a New Testament passage describing how Jesus fulfilled the given promise.

SOME BEGINNER'S TIPS

For those who may be new to Bible reading, new to Jesus or new to the Christian faith—maybe just checking out "this Jesus thing"—that's okay. Everybody has to start somewhere. Here are some tips as you begin your reading:

- Before you begin, ask God to lead you and guide you as you go through the material. It's never a bad idea to ask God—the source of all wisdom—for a little piece of wisdom.
- Read this book alongside an open Bible. Henrietta Mears is constantly asking you to look up Bible verses and passages, and the person who does so will gain immeasurably from the exercise. It takes patience and perseverance to look up all the passages referenced in this book. Mears believed in teaching key concepts through repetition, so sometimes she asks you to look up the same verses several times. My advice to you is this: If things are progressing too slowly, don't feel like you must look up every single reference. Just look up the ones that will help you understand.

Maybe you can take a pencil and check those you look up; then look up the others later if you have the time and inclination.

· Keep a Bible concordance nearby. To solidify her points, Mears occasionally asks you to look up certain words in a Bible concordance, an alphabetical list of all of the principal words in the Bible. This Bible study aid will help you find where words occur in the Bible and it is a great tool if you want to see how one word is used in different contexts. Nowadays, you can even find Bible concordances on computer software, which work even better than book concordances because of their extensive search capabilities.

Now it's time to discover *what Jesus is all about!*

Bayard Taylor
Senior Theological Editor
Gospel Light

UNDERSTANDING
THE GOSPELS

*The Gospels Portray Jesus Christ,
Our Savior and Lord*

Dr. Henry Van Dyke (1852-1933), Presbyterian minister and professor of English literature at Princeton, said:

> If four witnesses should appear before a judge to give an account of a certain event, and each should tell exactly the same story in the same words, the judge would probably conclude, not that their testimony was exceptionally valuable, but that the only event which was certain beyond a doubt was that they had agreed to tell the same story. But if each man had told what he

had seen, as he had seen it, then the evidence would be credible. And when we read the four Gospels, is not that exactly what we find? The four men tell the same story each in his own way.

The word "gospel" is derived from the two Anglo-Saxon words: "God," meaning "good," and "spell," meaning "tidings" or "history." The four writers of the Gospels are called evangelists; "evangelist" comes from a Greek word meaning "bringer of good tidings." The first three Gospels—Matthew, Mark and Luke—are called the Synoptic Gospels, because they closely follow each other in order of events. The word "synopsis" is derived from the two Greek words meaning "a view together, a collective view." Therefore, these three Gospels are striking in their similarities.

While the Synoptics focus on Christ's ministry in Galilee, John's Gospel stands in a class by itself. John hones in on Christ's ministry in Judea. The Synoptics narrate Christ's miracles, parables and addresses to the multitudes. John presents Christ's deeper and more abstract discourses, His conversations and His prayers. The three Synoptic Gospels portray Christ in action. John portrays Him in meditation and communion.

The most important fact proclaimed in all the Gospels is that Christ is here! The promised One has come! The One whom all the prophets have foretold, Jesus Christ, the Lord.

Every prophet in the Old Testament assured God's Chosen People again and again that a Messiah would come who would be the King of the Jews. The people looked forward with passionate longing and patriotism to the coming of that King in pomp and power:

The one Moses wrote about in the Law, and about whom the prophets also wrote—Jesus (John 1:45).

However, we will find Him infinitely more beautiful in person than in any prophet's vision of Him.

We read in Isaiah 7:14: "Therefore the Lord himself will give you a sign: The virgin will be with child and will give birth to a son, and will call him Immanuel." The name "Immanuel" means "God with us." This is the One the evangelists tell us about. The Gospels present Jesus in our midst. John says:

The Word became flesh and made his dwelling among us (1:14).

Think of it: God's coming down to live with people! It seems the Gospels are the center of the whole Bible. All that the prophets have said leads us to our Lord's earthly life and work; and all that follows in the Epistles proceeds from them. The Gospels are the source. Also notice where the four Gospels are placed. They stand at the close of the Old Testament and before the Epistles.

The Gospels tell us *when* and *how* Christ came.

The Epistles tell us *why* and *for what* Christ came.

WHAT IS THE GOSPEL?

"Gospel" means "good news." The good news concerning Jesus, the Son of God, is given to us by four writers—Matthew, Mark, Luke and John—although there is only one gospel, the glad story of salvation through Jesus Christ our Lord. When we speak of the Gospel of Luke, we are speaking of the good news of Jesus Christ as recorded by Luke. From the earliest times, the term "Gospel" has been applied to each of the four narratives that record the life of Christ.

No doubt, the good news originally was not presented in written form. Men went from one place to another, telling the glad story by word of mouth. After a while, a written record was necessary. More than one person attempted this, with no success:

> Many have undertaken to draw up an account of the things that have been fulfilled among us, just as they were handed down to us by those who from the first were eyewitnesses and servants of the word. Therefore, since I myself have carefully investigated everything from the beginning, it seemed good also to me to write an orderly account for you, most excellent Theophilus, so that you may know the certainty of the things you have been taught (Luke 1:1-4).

There is only one gospel but with four presentations that give us different angles of the story of Christ. The combined Gospel records set forth a personality rather than a connected life story.

WHY FOUR GOSPELS?

As everyone knows, there are four Gospels. But why four? Why wouldn't one straightforward, continuous narrative have been enough? Wouldn't one account have been simpler and clearer?

Wouldn't it have saved us from some of the difficulties in what some have said are conflicting accounts?

The answer seems plain: One or two accounts would *not* have given us a sufficient portrayal of the life of Christ. There are four distinct offices of Christ portrayed in the Gospels. He is presented as *King* (in Matthew), *servant* (in Mark), S*on of man* (in Luke) and *Son of God* (in John).

It is true that each of the four Gospels has much in common with the others. Each one deals with Christ's earthly ministry, His death and resurrection, and His teachings and miracles; but each Gospel has unique aspects as well. At once we see that each of the writers is trying to present a different picture of our Lord.

Matthew deliberately adds to his account what Mark omits. In fact, there is a lack of completeness about Jesus' life history in any one of the four Gospels. Read what John says:

> Jesus did many other things as well. If every one of them were written down, I suppose that even the whole world would not have room for the books that would be written (21:25).

Deliberate gaps exist that none of the evangelists professes to fill. For instance, all omit any account of the 18 years of Christ's life between the ages of 12 and 30.

Although each Gospel is complete in itself, each is very selective. Only a few of His miracles are described and only a portion of His teachings are given. Each evangelist has recorded that which is relevant and pertinent to his particular theme.

By seeing more than one perspective we better understand the whole picture. In the National Gallery in London, there are three representations on a single canvas of Charles I. In one picture, his head is turned to the right; in another, his head is turned to the left; and in the other, we find the full-face view. Anthony Van Dyck (1599-1641), the Flemish painter, painted them for Giovanni Lorenzo Bernini (1598-1680), the Roman sculptor, to help Bernini make a bust of the king. By combining the three impressions, Bernini would be better able to produce a "speaking" likeness. One view would not have been enough.

It may be true that the Gospels were intended to serve the very purpose that these portraits served. Each Gospel account presents a different aspect of our Lord's life on Earth. Together we have the complete picture. He is the King, but He is also the perfect servant. He is the Son of man, but we must not forget that He is the Son of God.

There are four Gospels with one Christ, four accounts with one purpose and four sketches of one person.

Dr. William H. Griffith Thomas (1861-1924), American New Testament scholar, gives the pictures of the Gospels in this way:

> Matthew is concerned with the coming of a *Promised Savior*.
> Mark is concerned with the life of a *Powerful Savior*.
> Luke is concerned with the grace of a *Perfect Savior*.
> John is concerned with the possession of a *Personal Savior*.

WHERE IS JESUS IN THE GOSPELS?

If we master the outline of Jesus as King, servant, Son of man, and Son of God, we will be familiar with the contents of the Gospels for life.

Fulfilled Old Testament Prophecies on the King Christ Jesus

He is the one who will build a house for my Name, and I will establish the throne of his kingdom forever. I will be his father, and he will be my son (2 Sam. 7:13-14).

For to us a child is born, to us a son is given, and the government will be on his shoulders. And he will be called Wonderful Counselor, Mighty God, Everlasting Father, Prince of Peace (Isa. 9:6).

All the Gospels are bound up with the promises of the Messiah in the Old Testament; the Gospels cannot be explained apart from the great messianic prophecies in the Old Testament. The prophets provided a magnificent picture of the Messiah. They told of His offices; His mission; and His birth, suffering, death, resurrection and glory. Let us consider some of the names and titles the prophets bestowed upon Him, as well as the main theme of each Gospel.

The King Christ Jesus

Matthew presents Jesus as King. This Gospel was written primarily for the Jews, because Christ is the Son of David. His royal genealogy is listed in Matthew 1:1-17. In Matthew 5—7, the Sermon on the Mount, we have the manifesto of the King, which contains the laws of His kingdom.

These passages, among many others, tell of the kingly

office of the Messiah: 2 Samuel 7:13-14; Psalm 72; Isaiah 9:6-7; Jeremiah 23:5; Zechariah 9:9; 14:9. The prophets tell us about His kingdom and its extent, and of Christ's ultimate triumph.

The Servant Christ Jesus

Mark depicts Jesus as servant. This Gospel was written to the Romans; and there is no genealogy. Why? People are not interested in the genealogy of a servant. More miracles are found here than in any other Gospel. The Romans cared little for words and far more for deeds.

These passages reflect the servant of Jehovah: Isaiah 42:1-7; 52:13-15; 53.

> **Fulfilled Old Testament Prophecies on the Servant Christ Jesus**
>
> *Here is my servant, whom I uphold, my chosen one in whom I delight; I will put my Spirit on him and he will bring justice to the nations (Isa. 42:1).*
>
> *But he was pierced for our transgressions, he was crushed for our iniquities; the punishment that brought us peace was upon him, and by his wounds we are healed (Isa. 53:5).*

The Man Christ Jesus

Luke sets forth Jesus as the perfect man. This Gospel was written to the Greeks and tells how Jesus' genealogy goes back to Adam, the first man, instead of beginning with Abraham, as did the Gospel written to the Jews. As a perfect man, Jesus is seen much in prayer and with angels who minister to Him.

He is called "Immanuel," which means "God with us"

(2 Sam. 7:14-16)—the "offspring" who would defeat Satan (Gen. 3:15); bring blessing and salvation to all nations (see Gen. 22:18); and establish an everlasting Kingdom (see 2 Sam. 7:14-16). Additional verses that reflect the Son of man include Psalm 8:4 (compare this to Hebrews 2:5-9) and Daniel 7:13.

The God-Man

John portrays Jesus as the Son of God. Written to all who will believe, with the purpose of leading people to Christ (see John 20:31), everything in this Gospel illustrates and demonstrates His divine relationship. The opening verse carries us back to the beginning of creation.

Jesus is called God or Lord in the following verses: Isaiah 9:6; 40:3-5; 47:4; Jeremiah 23:6.

WHAT TYPES OF PEOPLE TODAY ARE LIKE THE PEOPLE IN JESUS' DAY?

Christ was presented to widely different types of people who made up the world. Each group of people was capable of appreciating one particular kind of presentation more than another. Additionally, the four groups of people in Jesus' day represent four types of people today.

Jewish People

The Jewish people had special training. They were steeped in the Old Testament Scripture and the prophets. Matthew wrote the story of Jesus' life, especially for these people. If Jewish people were to be impressed with Jesus, they would need to be taught by someone who understood their customs and way of thinking. Jewish people needed to know that Jesus came to fulfill the prophecies of the Old Testament. Over and over again we read: "And so was fulfilled what the Lord had said through the prophet" (Matt. 2:15).

We have the same type of people today. They revel in prophecies fulfilled and unfulfilled. They seek to know what the prophets spoke and how the prophecies were brought to pass.

Romans

Mark wrote especially for the Romans, masters of the world at that time. The Romans knew nothing about Old Testament Scripture. They were not interested in prophecy being fulfilled, yet they were vitally concerned about a remarkable leader who had appeared in Palestine—Jesus. He claimed more than ordinary authority and possessed extraordinary powers. They wanted to hear more about this Jesus—what sort of a person He really was, what He said and what He had done.

The Romans liked Mark's straightforward message. To advance the story rapidly, the word "and" is used in Mark 1,375 times (*KJV*). Mark's Gospel moves on in a beauty and force all its own. It is filled with deeds, not words. Clearly it is the Gospel of the ministry of Christ.

The Romans of Jesus' day were like today's average businesspeople. Men and women in the marketplace are not concerned at first about the genealogy of a king but with a God who is able—a God who can meet a person's every need. Mark is the businessperson's Gospel.

Greeks

Luke, the Greek doctor, wrote for the people of his own country, who were lovers of beauty, poetry and culture. The Greeks lived in a world of large ideas. Their tastes were fastidious. The Gospel of Luke tells of the birth and childhood of Jesus. It gives the inspired songs connected with the life of Christ. We find the salutation of Elizabeth when Mary visited her (see Luke 1:42-45). We hear the song of the virgin mother (see vv. 46-55). Even Zechariah burst into praise when speech was restored to him (see vv. 68-79). At the Savior's birth, a chorus of angel voices rang out (see Luke 2:13-14), and then the shepherd's song of praise to God was heard (see v. 20).

The Greeks of Jesus' day were like today's students and idealists who are seeking after truth, for they believe that truth is the means to happiness.

All People

John's Gospel is written for all people everywhere so that they might believe that Jesus is the Christ. John portrayed Christ as the Son of God. This Gospel is filled with extraordinary claims that attest to Jesus' divine character and mission.

The "all people" of John's day were like the masses today who need Christ. They include anyone who will believe on the Lord Jesus because they have a sense of need and want to receive the gift of eternal life through Jesus Christ the Lord.

WHAT ARE THE KEYS TO THE GOSPELS?

Front-Door Keys

God has hung the key to the Gospel of Matthew right over the entrance. The book opens: "A record of the genealogy of Jesus Christ the son of David, the son of Abraham" (Matt. 1:1). This shows Jesus' covenant position as the Son of Abraham (see Gen. 12:1-3; Gal. 3:16) and His royal position as the Son of David.

Matthew presents Christ as King; he gives the royal genealogy in the first 17 verses. A king is not chosen by popular ballot but by birth.

Turn now to Mark and see how this book opens. No genealogy is given because Mark portrays Jesus as a servant, and no one is interested in the pedigree of a servant.

Turn to Luke. Is a genealogy given (see Luke 3:23-27)? While Matthew traces Christ's line back to Abraham and David to show He was a Jew and of the royal line, Luke traces His line back to Adam. Christ is presented as the ideal man.

Turn to John. How does this book open? There is no genealogy; instead we read: "In the beginning was the Word, and the Word was with God, and the Word was God" (1:1). Christ is portrayed as God in John.

Backdoor Keys

Now let us see how the Gospels close. Turn to Matthew 28:18-20. Here the King commands and commissions His disciples. The Messiah is still on Earth, for it is on Earth and not in heaven that the Son of David shall reign in glory.

> All authority in heaven and on earth has been given to me. Therefore go and make disciples of all nations, baptizing them in the name of the Father and of the Son and of the Holy Spirit, and teaching them to obey everything I have commanded you. And surely I am with you always, to the very end of the age.

Now look at the close of Mark. It is very significant and appropriate: "Then the disciples went out and preached everywhere, and the Lord worked with them and confirmed his word by the signs that accompanied it" (16:20). Jesus, the servant, is pictured as still laboring with His disciples.

Luke ends in a different way. Jesus, the perfect man, is ascending to the Father. Notice what Luke says in 24:51: "While he was blessing them, he left them and was taken up into heaven."

The closing verse of John is also significant: "Jesus did many other things as well. If every one of them were written down, I suppose that even the whole world would not have room for the books that would be written" (21:25). Truly, "no one ever spoke the way this man does" (7:46), for He is the very Son of God.

STUDY GUIDE

In this study, Henrietta Mears urges us to consider the significance of the four accounts of Jesus' life written by Matthew, Mark, Luke and John. First, read through this whole book, and then come back to answer the questions in this study guide.

THE FOUR GOSPELS

1. Why are Matthew, Mark, Luke and John called evangelists?

2. Why would the news about Jesus be thought of as good news?

3. What is the difference between the four Gospels and the gospel as a whole?

4. Why do you think there are four Gospels and not just one Gospel?

GOD'S PROMISE

A crucial concept in understanding the Gospels is God's promise to His Chosen People, the Jews, to send them a Messiah, or messianic deliverer. Let's examine some of the prominent passages of Scripture along these lines and compare them to various messianic expectations.

5. The word "Messiah" comes from the Hebrew word "to anoint." In the Old Testament, God anointed (i.e., set apart) kings and prophets for special service. The word "Christ" comes from the Greek word also meaning "to anoint." When the New Testament speaks of Jesus Christ, "Christ" is not Jesus' last name; instead, the meaning is "Jesus the Anointed One, the Promised Messiah." Given what we have discovered so far, what would you expect God's anointed Messiah to do?

6. Read Matthew 3:7-12, which speaks of John the Baptist's confrontation with some religious leaders. When he sees many of the Pharisees and Sadducees coming to where he is baptizing, he says:

What kind of Messiah was John the Baptist expecting?

7. In 2 Samuel 7:13-14, God makes a promise to King David about the coming Messiah: "He is the one who will build a house for my Name, and I will establish the throne of his kingdom forever. I will be his father, and he will be my son." (This was written about one thousand years before Jesus' birth.) Now read Matthew 22:42. What kind of Messiah were the disciples expecting?

Now read Matthew 9:27; 12:23; 15:22. What kind of Messiah were these hurting people expecting?

Finally, read Matthew 21:9, which describes Jesus' wild entry into Jerusalem just before He was betrayed and crucified. What kind of Messiah were the common people expecting?

8. In a passage written over seven hundred years before Jesus' birth, Isaiah 53:4-6 says of the coming messianic servant:

> Surely he took up our infirmities and carried our sorrows, yet we considered him stricken by God, smitten by him, and afflicted. But he was pierced for our transgressions, he was crushed for our iniquities; the punishment that brought us peace was upon him, and by his wounds we are healed. We all, like sheep, have gone astray, each of us has turned to his own way; and the LORD has laid on him the iniquity of us all.

Compare this passage of Scripture to Matthew 8:16-17. How did Jesus fulfill Isaiah's vision?

John 19:34 describes the crucifixion scene: "Instead, one of the soldiers pierced Jesus' side with a spear, bringing a sudden flow of blood and water." This piercing of the Messiah is also mentioned in Zechariah 12:10. What expectations do these passages convey about the Messiah?

9. Genesis 22:18 is God's irrevocable oath to Abraham that He would follow through on an earlier promise (see Gen. 12:1-3)—that "through your offspring all nations on earth will be blessed." Blessing in the Bible includes at the very least reconciliation, friendship and fellowship with God.

   Compare the verses above to Luke 24:47. How did Jesus' coming as Messiah fulfill God's promise to Abraham two thousand years earlier?

10. Daniel 7:13-14 identifies an incredible messianic figure. Compare Daniel's vision to what Jesus said about Himself in Mark 13:26. According to this verse, what did Jesus expect of Himself as Messiah?

11. Jeremiah 23:6 says that the Messiah will be called "The LORD Our Righteousness."

    "Lord" as a name is very common in the Gospels (see Matt. 8:2,6,8,21,25; Mark 1:3; 2:28; 7:28; 9:24; 16:19; Luke 2:11; 5:8,12; 6:46; John 4:3; 6:23,28). Why is it so remarkable that Jesus' disciples—trained as Jews since infancy to worship the one true God alone—would self-consciously call Jesus Lord?

12. How can we account for all these different expectations for the coming One who was promised by God? The Bible actually portrays *two* comings of the Messiah: the first at a strategic, historical point in time

as a servant and Savior, and the second at the end of this present age as a conquering King who brings peace to Earth. Review the various expectations and try to determine whether they refer to first or second coming, or something of a combined expectation.

13. For the sake of argument, let's assume that what the Gospel writers say about Jesus is true and that you believe it is true. What difference does your belief make in your life?

CHAPTER 2

UNDERSTANDING matthew

Matthew Portrays Jesus Christ, the Promised Messiah

Matthew wrote with a special goal in mind. His Gospel showed the Jews that Jesus is their long-expected Messiah, the Son of David, and that His life fulfilled the Old Testament prophecies. The purpose is stated in Matthew 1:1: "A record of the genealogy of Jesus Christ the son of David, the son of Abraham." This statement links Christ with two of the great covenants God made with David and Abraham. God's covenant with David consisted of the promise of a king to sit upon his throne forever (see 2 Sam. 7:8-13). God's covenant with Abraham promised that through him all families of the earth would be blessed (see Gen. 12:3). David's son was a king.

Abraham's son was a sacrifice. Matthew opens with the birth of the King and closes with the offering of a sacrifice.

From the beginning of Matthew's Gospel, Jesus is associated with the Jewish nation. Matthew used wisdom in not alienating the Jews who might read the story. He convinces them that in the person and kingdom of Jesus, God fulfilled every prophecy spoken concerning their promised Messiah. He quotes freely from the Old Testament—more than any of the other evangelists (29 quotations are given). Thirteen times he says that this or that event took place "to fulfill what the Lord had said through the prophet" (Matt. 1:22).

It may be difficult for us to appreciate how great is the transition from the old to the new. It seemed to the Jews that they must give up their tradition and orthodoxy and accept another creed. Matthew, in his Gospel, shows the Jewish believers in Jesus that they were not giving up their old faith but rather accepting its fulfillment in Jesus (Paul's writings, especially Galatians, have the same theme).

MATTHEW REVEALED

Matthew was well acquainted with Jewish history and customs. He spoke of farming and fishing and housekeeping in the seven parables (see Matt. 13). These were areas that would strike a responsive chord in the hearts of the Jewish people.

As we read Matthew, we get a clear and comprehensive view of the entire Gospel. We should note the balance between Jesus' ministry and teaching. We find the genealogy of the King, His birth in Bethlehem—the city of David—according to Micah's prophecy (see Mic. 5:2); the coming of the forerunner,

John the Baptist, as Malachi predicted (see Mal. 3:1); the ministry of the King; His rejection by Israel; and the promise of His coming again in power and glory.

The author of this Gospel is no doubt a Jewish believer in Jesus (see Matt. 9:9; 10:3). Matthew, whose name means "gift of the Lord," was a tax collector at Capernaum, a city under the Roman control, when Jesus chose him as one of the 12 disciples. His name is found in all the lists of the Twelve, though Mark and Luke give his other name, Levi. The only word the author speaks about himself is that he was a "publican" (see Matt. 10:3, *KJV*), which was a term of reproach in much the same way the term "politician" is today. The other evangelists tell about the great feast Matthew gave Jesus, so no doubt Matthew was a man of means. Mark and Luke also, though, record the significant fact that Matthew left all and followed Jesus.

JESUS REVEALED

Matthew breaks the silence of four hundred years between Malachi's prophecy—in the last book of the Old Testament—and the announcement of the birth of Jesus. At that time, Israel was under the domination of the Roman Empire. No man of the house of David had been allowed to sit upon the throne for six hundred years.

Herod was not a true king of Israel; he was a governor of Judea, appointed by the emperor of Rome. The man who really had the right to the throne of the house of David was Joseph, the carpenter who became the husband of Mary. (See the genealogy of Joseph in Matthew 1 and notice especially one name, Jeconiah, in verse 11.) If Joseph had been Jesus' father according to the flesh, Jesus could never have occupied the throne, for God's Word barred the way. There had been a curse on this royal line since the days of Jeconiah. In Jeremiah 22:30, we read:

> This is what the LORD says: "Record this man as if childless, a man who will not prosper in his lifetime, for none of his offspring will prosper, none will sit on the throne of David or rule anymore in Judah."

Joseph was in the line of this curse. Hence, if Christ had been Joseph's son, He could not have sat on David's throne.

We find another genealogy in Luke 3. This is Mary's line back to David through Nathan, not Jeconiah (see Luke 3:31). There was no curse on this line. To Mary, God said:

> Do not be afraid, Mary, you have found favor with God. You will be with child and give birth to a son, and you are to give him the name Jesus. He will be great and will be called the Son of the Most High. The Lord God will give him the throne of his father David, and he will reign over the house of Jacob forever; his kingdom will never end (Luke 1:30-33).

Now the silence had been broken, and the coming of the Messiah had been declared.

COMING OF THE KING (MATTHEW 1—2)

Matthew is the Gospel of the Messiah, God's anointed One. The main theme of this book is to show that Jesus of Nazareth is the predicted Messiah, the deliverer of whom Moses and the prophets wrote: "whose origins are from of old, from ancient times" (Mic. 5:2). He is the child that was to be born, the Son given, of whom Isaiah speaks: "Wonderful Counselor, Mighty God, Everlasting Father, Prince of Peace" (Isa. 9:6).

The maps of the world and the calendars of time tell of Christ's birthplace and birthday. Jesus was born in Bethlehem of Judea (see Mic. 5:2; Matt. 2:1), in the days of Herod the king. We know this place and this king. We don't have to build the story out of our imagination, because Christianity is a historical religion. The Gospel does not begin with "Once upon a time"; it starts with "Bethlehem in Judea" (Matt. 2:1). The town is real, so we know the very place where Jesus was born. And the time is definite: "during the time of King Herod" (Matt. 2:1). History knows Herod. There is nothing mythical about it.

These are facts that no critic or unbeliever can doubt. The Gospel narrative sets its record on the solid foundation of history. Jesus' coming was not hidden; it was public knowledge unafraid of the geographer's map or the historian's pen.

Genealogies of Christ

The story of the birth of Jesus in Matthew differs from the record in Luke, but both records complement one another. Jesus' earthly life began in a stable. His cradle was a manger. His family and associates were humble folks. He came as a helpless human babe, yet Jesus was heralded by an archangel, welcomed by an angel choir and worshiped by Earth's wisest philosophers. At the same time, Jesus was both human *and* divine!

Most young people, when they begin reading Matthew's

Old Testament Promise and New Testament Fulfillment

Therefore the Lord himself will give you a sign: The virgin will be with child and will give birth to a son, and will call him Immanuel (Isa. 7:14).

All this took place to fulfill what the Lord had said through the prophet: "The virgin will be with child and will give birth to a son, and they will call him Immanuel"—which means, "God with us" (Matt. 1:22-23).

"begats" (see *KJV*) and Luke's "the son of's," wonder what these are all about. We ought to realize that if they were included in Scripture, they were put there purposefully. Therefore, we should further explore these two genealogies.

A genealogy is "the history of the descent of an individual or family from an ancestor."[1] The first genealogy of Christ in Scripture is found in Matthew 1:1-17 and the second is in Luke 3:23-38. They are not alike—each traces the descent of Christ for different purposes.

Matthew traces Jesus' line back to Abraham and David to show that He was a Jew of the royal line of David. Luke traces Jesus' line back to Adam to show that He belonged to the human race.

Matthew shows Jesus as the King, the Messiah, the lion of the tribe of Judah and the promised ruler of Israel. Luke shows Jesus as coming from human lineage—the ideal man born of woman. You will find that these pictures of Jesus are maintained through each Gospel.

Why are we concerned about these genealogies? Because they give us the key to the whole life of Christ. They show us from the very start that He was not just another man; He was descended from a royal family—a king's blood ran through His veins. If He were not a king, then He could not claim the rulership of our lives. And if He were not man, He could not know our sorrows and understand our griefs.

Trail of Christ

Read through Matthew and follow this trail of the King:

Old Testament Promise and New Testament Fulfillment

But you, Bethlehem Ephrathah, though you are small among the clans of Judah, out of you will come for me one who will be ruler over Israel, whose origins are from of old, from ancient times (Mic. 5:2).

When he had called together all the people's chief priests and teachers of the law, he asked them where the Christ was to be born. "In Bethlehem in Judea," they replied, "for this is what the prophet has written" (Matt. 2:4-5).

- *A King's name*—" 'They will call him Immanuel'—which means, 'God with us' " (1:23).
- *A King's position*—"For out of you will come a ruler who will be the shepherd of my people Israel" (2:6).
- *A King's announcement*—"Prepare the way for the Lord, make straight paths for him" (3:3).
- *A King's coronation*—"This is my Son, whom I love; with him I am well pleased" (3:17).
- *A King's proclamation*—"and he began to teach them" (5:2); "he taught as one who had authority" (7:29).
- *A King's loyalty*—"He who is not with me is against

Old Testament Promise and New Testament Fulfillment

I will proclaim the decree of the LORD: He said to me, "You are my Son; today I have become your Father" (Ps. 2:7).

And a voice from heaven said, "This is my Son, whom I love; with him I am well pleased" (Matt. 3:17).

me, and he who does not gather with me scatters" (12:30).

• *A King's enemies*—"From that time on Jesus began to explain to his disciples that he must go to Jerusalem and suffer many things at the hands of the elders, chief priests and teachers of the law" (16:21).

• *A King's love*—"the Son of man did not come to be served, but to serve, and to give his life as a ransom for many" (20:28).

• *A King's glory*—"When the Son of man comes . . . then the King will say . . . 'Come, you who are blessed by my Father; take your inheritance' " (25:31-34).

• *A King's sacrifice*—"When they had crucified him . . . they placed the written charge against him: THIS IS JESUS, THE KING OF THE JEWS" (27:35-37).

• *A King's victory*—"He is not here; he has risen, just as he said" (28:6).

Matthew alone tells of the visit of the wise men from the East. These were Persian magi, scholars and students of the stars. They came to worship and honor a king. These wise men did not come inquiring about the whereabouts of the Savior of the world. Instead, they asked, "Where is the one who has been born king of the Jews?" (2:2).

Mark, Luke and John are silent about the wise men because their records do not record the birth of a king. The holy, sacred star halted over a manger in Bethlehem to tell of Christ's birth. The whole world at this time was expecting the advent of some great One. Where is the One who has been born king of the Jews? was the question on every lip. With all the prophecies that had been made to Israel, neither the world nor Israel could be criticized for expecting a king who would rule the earth from David's throne (see Isa. 9:7; Jer. 23:3-6; 30:8-10; 33:14-16,25-26; Ezek. 37:21; Hos. 3:4-5).

Old Testament Promise and New Testament Fulfillment

He will rule from sea to sea and from the River to the ends of the earth (Ps. 72:8).

That at the name of Jesus every knee should bow, in heaven and on earth and under the earth, and every tongue confess that Jesus Christ is Lord, to the glory of God the Father (Phil. 2:10-11).

The priests knew where Christ was to be born, but they did not know Christ when He was born.

The wise men were led to a person, not a creed.

The adoration of the wise men foreshadowed Christ's universal dominion. Some day "every knee should bow . . . and every tongue confess that Jesus Christ is Lord, to the glory of God the Father" (Phil. 2:10-11), and "he will rule from sea to sea and from the River to the ends of the earth" (Ps. 72:8).

Paul tells us in Galatians 4:4-5:

> But when the time had fully come, God sent his Son, born of a woman, born under law, to redeem those under law, that we might receive the full rights of sons.

Jesus came to be the world's Savior.

The birth of Jesus was followed by approximately 12 years of silence until His visit with the doctors in Jerusalem (see Luke 2:45-47). Then silence followed again. Only the reference to Jesus being a carpenter (see Matt. 13:55; Mark 6:3) throws any light upon what Jesus was doing for the next 18 years. Jesus took 30 years of preparation for three years of ministry.

PROCLAMATION OF THE KINGDOM (MATTHEW 3—16:20)

John the Baptist had another name. As the prophet Isaiah began to unfold the real message of his book—the coming of the Messiah, servant of Jehovah—he introduced a character known simply as a voice:

> A voice of one calling: "In the desert prepare the way for the LORD; make straight in the wilderness a highway for our God" (Isa. 40:3).

This voice, although unnamed here, is to be the herald of Jesus Christ. His two functions—that of voice and that of messenger (see Mal. 3:1)—are all that the Old Testament tells us of John the Baptist. But it is a lot. Not only was Christ foretold all through the Scriptures, but also His forerunner, John the Baptist, was described!

In Matthew, we again hear the voice:

"Repent, for the kingdom of heaven is near." This is he who was spoken of through the prophet Isaiah: "A voice of one calling in the desert, 'Prepare the way for the Lord, make straight paths for him'" (3:2-3).

The King must be announced! It was the herald's duty to go before the king, like a Roman officer before his ruler, and command that the roads be repaired over which his master would travel. John the Baptist did this for the Christ. He showed that the spiritual roads of the lives of men, women and nations were full of sin's potholes and needed rebuilding and straightening.

We then see the King stepping from His personal and private life into His public ministry (see Matt. 4) and into a crisis. Satan met Him after the benediction of the Father at His baptism: "This is my Son, whom I love; with him I am well pleased" (Matt. 3:17). When Jesus went forth to carry out the plans for which He had come into the world, He was led into the wilderness to face the first major conflict of His public ministry.

Notice that Satan offered Jesus a shortcut to that universal kingdom Jesus would gain through the long and painful way of the cross. Jesus Christ came to be Savior first, and then King. How strong is the temptation to take a shortcut to our ambitions (see 1 Cor. 10:13)! Yet Jesus stood victorious against Satan, His shield undented and untarnished. He overcame all subsequent temptations until His final victory and ascension to heaven as Lord of all.

The Kingdom Laws

Every kingdom has laws and standards to enable it to exercise authority over its subjects. The kingdom of heaven is no exception. Jesus declared that He came not to destroy the Law but to fulfill it (see Matt. 5:17). The old Law was good in its day. Moses and the prophets were far in advance of their time; they were pioneers. Jesus did not destroy this old Law, but He did treat it as law that was not perfect and final (see Heb. 8:13).

Jesus' message is that any reform that starts on the outside and works its way in begins on the wrong side. Christ starts on the inside and works out. The only way to get a good life is to first get a good heart.

From the lofty pulpit of a mountain, Jesus preached the Sermon on the Mount, which contains the laws of His kingdom (see Matt. 5—7). Let's read through these chapters and freshen our memories about this most wonderful of Jesus' discourses. After more than two thousand years, the Sermon on the Mount has lost none of its majesty or power. Its teachings surpass all human teachings. The world has not yet caught up with its simplistic ideals and requirements.

Many a person who is not a Christian claims that the Sermon on the Mount is his or her religion. How little this person understands the depth of that sermon's meaning! It is important that we don't simply praise what Jesus said as a wonderful theory but that we actually practice it in our own lives. If we let this rule operate in our lives, it will change our personal relations, heal our social wounds and solve every dispute between nations—yes, it will set the whole world in order. The root of this law is kindness. If human society would set the Sermon on the Mount's standards as law, the world would be set in order—every day filled with kindness, which would be a taste of heaven. Love would reign instead of lawlessness. Christ shows us that sin lies not just in committing the act but also in the motive behind it (see Matt. 5:21-22,27-29). No one can expect forgiveness who does not forgive (see Matt. 6:12,14-15). Has anyone yet ever fathomed the depth of Matthew 7:12? It is easy to read but hard to do.

Jesus preached that "the kingdom of heaven is near" (Matt. 3:2; 4:17; 10:7) or "at hand" (*KJV*). He set forth the condition for entrance to the kingdom, its laws, its privileges and its rewards. The Sermon on the Mount serves as the Constitution of the Kingdom. Fourteen times the King says: "I tell you." (Let's find and mark these instances in our Bibles.) These words reveal Jesus' authority as He dealt with the Law of Moses. He told the people that they must not only keep the Law outwardly but also keep it in spirit. Notice the effect of His words on the people:

> When Jesus had finished saying these things, the crowds were amazed at his teaching, because he taught as one who had authority, and not as their teachers of the law (Matt. 7:28-29).

The King's Power

We find that the King met human needs through the work of amazing miracles (see Matt. 8—9). There are 12 miracles recorded in these chapters. After Jesus had performed the miracles, "All the people were astonished and said, 'Could this be the Son of David?'" (Matt. 12:23). The scribes, however, passed their hostile judgment on the actions of Jesus (see Matt. 9:3).

Still, the Kingdom was proclaimed "at hand" because the King Himself was there.

The King's Cabinet

Jesus not only preached Himself, but He also gathered others around Him to carry out His work. It was necessary to organize His kingdom in order to establish it on a wider and more permanent basis. Just as a king must have subjects, Jesus reflected His light through human instruments. He said to His followers, "You are the light of the world" (Matt. 5:14). Jesus still has a great message for the world and He still needs us to carry it to that world. Spiritual ideas cannot walk alone and be of any value. They must be clothed with men, women and institutions who will serve as the heart and brain, hands and feet to carry out His message. This is what Jesus did when He walked on Earth; He called men and women into His companionship to train them to carry on His work.

Where did Jesus find His helpers? Not in the Temple among the doctors or priests and not in the colleges of Jerusalem. He found His helpers on the seashore mending their nets. Jesus did not call many of the mighty or noble; rather, He chose the foolish things of the world to confound the wise (see 1 Cor. 1:27).

A list of the disciples is given in Matthew 10:2-4. This is probably the most important catalog of names in the world, names of men who had been given a work to do that would make winning battles and founding empires seem small in comparison. We find that their great message was the kingdom of heaven; their tremendous mission was to start it:

As you go, preach this message: "The kingdom of heaven is near" (Matt. 10:7).

Note some of the warnings and instructions for the disciples Jesus stated in Matthew 10. What are they? If these requirements of discipleship hold true today, would you call yourself a disciple? Thoughtfully consider Christ's words in Matthew 10:32-33.

The Kingdom of Heaven

The word "kingdom" occurs some 55 times in Matthew, for this is the Gospel of the King. The expression "kingdom of heaven" is found 35 times in Matthew and nowhere else in the Gospels. Of the 15 parables recorded in Matthew, all but three begin, "The kingdom of heaven is like."

Jewish people understood the term "kingdom of heaven." Neither Jesus nor John felt necessary to define it. At Sinai, God said to Israel, "You will be for me a kingdom of priests and a holy nation" (Exod. 19:6). Israel at first was a theocracy. God was their King; Israel formed His kingdom. The prophets had referred to the messianic kingdom again and again.

In His parables (see Matt. 13), Jesus likened the kingdom of heaven to the following:

- The sower
- The weeds
- A mustard seed
- Yeast in the dough
- A hidden treasure
- A pearl of great value
- A net

These parables, called "the knowledge of the secrets of the

kingdom of heaven" (Matt. 13:11), describe the result of the presence of Christ's gospel in the world during this present age until the time of His return when He will gather the harvest (see vv. 40-43). We see no bright picture of a converted world. Weeds will be mixed with the wheat, good fish with bad, yeast in the loaf. (Yeast, or leaven, is often a symbol of sin. The Spirit never uses yeast as a source of goodness.) Then there is an abnormal growth of the mustard seed that admits "birds of the air" to lodge in its branches (Matt. 13:32). This is Christendom. Only Christ can determine what is good and what is bad; and at the harvest, He will divide the two. If we are to have a kingdom on this earth, with the laws Christ set down, then we must have the King. Some day Christ will come in power and great glory and establish His throne on Earth. We will have peace when the Prince of Peace reigns!

REJECTION OF THE KING (MATTHEW 16:21–20)

The sad story reads that Christ "came to that which was his own, but his own did not receive him" (John 1:11). The gospel of the Kingdom was first preached to those who should have been most prepared—the children of Israel. And although many came to believe in Jesus as Messiah, as a whole the people rejected their King. Beginning in Matthew 12, we see much controversy among the leaders concerning Jesus.

Jesus announced that the Kingdom should be taken away from the Jewish people and given to another nation:

Therefore I tell you that the kingdom of God will be

taken away from you and given to a people who will produce its fruit (Matt. 21:43).

The announcement offended the rulers and "they looked for a way to arrest him" (v. 46).

Our Lord told Nicodemus, one of the religious leaders, the requirement for entrance into the kingdom of heaven (see John 3:3-7,16). Whoever believes may enjoy its privileges and blessings. The Kingdom is for the Gentile as well as the Jew.

Why did the Jewish leaders and many of the people refuse the Kingdom? The world today is longing intensely for the golden age. A millennium of peace and rest is the great desire of diplomats and rulers, but they want it in their own way and on their own terms. They desire to bring it about by their own efforts. They have no longing for a millennium brought about by the personal return of the Lord Jesus Christ. It was just so with the people in the days of John the Baptist.

Have you put Christ on the throne of your life? Do you have the peace you long for? Have you accepted Christ's terms for your life?

The Church Promised

We find Jesus with His disciples up north in Caesarea Philippi, apparently with the goal of having a private interview with them in which He would disclose a great truth (see Matt. 16:13-28).

Only in Matthew's Gospel is the Church named. After the Kingdom was rejected by the Jews, we find a change in the teachings of Jesus. He began to talk about the Church instead of the Kingdom (see v. 18). "Church" comes from the word *ecclesia*, which means "called out ones." Because all would not believe in Him, Christ said He was calling out anyone, Jew or Gentile, to belong to His Church—His body. He began to build a new edifice, a new body of people, which would include both Jews and Gentiles (see Eph. 2:14-18).

Life's Most Important Question

When Jesus and His disciples were far away from the busy scene in which they lived, Jesus asked His disciples, "Who do people say the Son of Man is?" (Matt. 16:13).

This is the important question today! First asked by an obscure Galilean in far-off solitude, it has thundered down through the centuries and become the mightiest question in the world today: What do you think of Christ? What we think of Him determines what we do and who we are. The ideas we hold about industry, wealth, government, morals and religion mold society and alter lives. Therefore, what we think of Christ today influences our lives and thoughts more than anything else.

The disciples gave the answers others were giving. The answers then were as varied as they are now: Jesus was an extraordinary person; He was a prophet; He was a person who had an element of the supernatural about Him. People's opinions of Christ are high.

Life's Most Important Answer

Jesus turned the general question into the sharp personal inquiry: "But whom say ye that I am?" (Matt. 16:15, *KJV*). We must each ask ourself this question. Important as the general question is, the personal question is far more important to each one of us. We cannot escape it. A neutral answer is impossible.

We must believe that Jesus is God or that He's an impostor.

"You are the Christ, the Son of the living God" exclaimed the impulsive, fervent Peter (Matt. 16:16). His response revealed that he grasped Christ as the Messiah—the fulfillment of the prophecies of the old Hebrew prophets. This confession was great because it exalted Christ as the Son of God; it lifted Him above humanity and crowned Him with deity. From then on, Jesus revealed to His handful of disciples new truths about His teachings. He then said to Peter and the disciples, "On this rock I will build my church" (v. 18). This was what Christ was going to do—build a Church of which He Himself was to be "the chief cornerstone" (Eph. 2:20). This Church was born on Pentecost (see Acts 2).

For the first time, the fateful shadow of the Cross fell across the path of the disciples. From this point on, Jesus began to draw back the curtain that veiled the future, showing His disciples what would come to pass. He saw His path running to Jerusalem and into the awful hatred of the priests and Pharisees, and then to the terrible Cross; but He also saw the glory of the resurrection morning (see Matt. 16:21).

Jesus did not reveal these things until His disciples were ready to bear them. God in His mercy often hides the future from us.

TRIUMPH OF THE KING
(MATTHEW 21—28)

On the morning of Palm Sunday, there was a stir in Bethany and along the road leading to Jerusalem. It was understood that Jesus was to enter the city that day. The people were gathering in crowds. A colt was procured, and the disciples, having thrown their robes over it, placed Jesus upon it, and the procession started. This little parade could not be compared in magnificence to any procession that has attended the coronation of a king or the inauguration of a president, but it meant much more for the world. Jesus, for the first time, permitted a public recognition and celebration of His rights as Messiah-King. The end was approaching with awful swiftness and He had to offer Himself as Messiah, even if only to be rejected.

In their enthusiasm, the people tore off branches from palm and olive trees and carpeted the highway, while shouts rang through the air. They believed in Jesus and, with all their warm enthusiasm, were not ashamed of their King. In answer to the crowds who asked, "Who is this?" they boldly answered, "This is the prophet, Jesus, from Nazareth of Galilee" (see Matt. 21:10-11). It took courage to say that in Jerusalem. Jesus was not entering the city as a triumphant conqueror, as the Romans had done. No sword was in His hand. Over Him floated no bloodstained banner. His mission was salvation!

In the evening, the crowds dispersed and Jesus quietly returned to Bethany. Apparently nothing in the way of making Jesus their King had been accomplished. His kingdom came without observation or pageantry. His hour had not yet come. Christ must be Savior first; then He would come again one day as King of kings and Lord of lords.

Christ's authority was brought into question as He went into the Temple and ordered the merchants out, overturning their tables and telling them that they had made the house of God a den of thieves. A bitter controversy followed. "Then the

Pharisees went out and laid plans to trap him in his words" (Matt. 22:15). He bade farewell to Jerusalem until He would come again to sit on David's throne.

THE FUTURE OF THE KINGDOM (24—25)

Much of Jesus' discourse in Matthew 24—25 is devoted to Christ's second coming. In the parables of the faithful servant (see 24:45-51), the 10 virgins (see 25:1-13) and the talents (see 25:14-30), He exhorts us to be ready.

When Jesus delivered His Mount of Olives discourse, He foretold the condition of the world after His ascension until He comes in glory to judge the nations according to their treatment of His brothers—the Jewish people (see Matt. 25:31-46). This is not the judgment of the great white throne, which is the judgment of the wicked dead (see Rev. 20:11-15). Neither is it the judgment seat of Christ, which is the judgment of saints according to their works (see 2 Cor. 5:10). It is the judgment of Gentile nations concerning their attitude toward God's people.

The Death and Resurrection of the King

We have passed through some of the highlights in the life of Jesus; now we step into the shadows as we enter Gethsemane. We see the Son of Abraham, the sacrifice, dying so that all the nations of the earth might be blessed by Him. Jesus was slain because He claimed to be the King of Israel; He was raised from the dead because He was the King (see Acts 2:30-36). Although a large number of disciples believed in Jesus and followed Him, the religious leaders' opposition was bitter, and they determined to put Him to death. On the

Old Testament Promise and New Testament Fulfillment

Roaring lions tearing their prey open their mouths wide against me . . . a band of evil men has encircled me, they have pierced my hands and my feet . . . people stare and gloat over me (Ps. 22:13,16-17).

Two robbers were crucified with him, one on his right and one on his left. Those who passed by hurled insults at him, shaking their heads and saying, "You who are going to destroy the temple and build it in three days, save yourself! Come down from the cross, if you are the Son of God!" (Matt. 27:38-40).

grounds of blasphemy and of claiming to be the King of the Jews—thus making Himself the enemy of the Roman emperor—Jesus was delivered by Pilate to be crucified.

Matthew is not alone in his record of the terrible circumstances of the Savior's passion, but he makes us feel that in the mock array—the crown of thorns, the scepter, the title over the cross—we have a witness, although it is one of scorn, to the kingly claim.

After hanging on the cross for six hours, the Savior died, not from physical suffering alone, but also of a broken heart, for He bore the sins of the whole world. We hear His triumphant cry, "It is finished" (John 19:30) when he had paid the debt of sin and became the world's redeemer!

The Great Price of Redemption

The mode of the Messiah's death had been foreshadowed by various stories and symbols in the Old Testament. The brass serpent in the wilderness signified that He was to be lifted up (see Num. 21:8-9); the lamb upon the Temple altar

Old Testament Promise

This is how you are to eat it: with your cloak tucked into your belt, your sandals on your feet and your staff in your hand. Eat it in haste; it is the LORD's Passover. On that same night I will pass through Egypt and strike down every firstborn—both men and animals—and I will bring judgment on all the gods of Egypt. I am the LORD. The blood will be a sign for you on the houses where you are; and when I see the blood, I will pass over you. No destructive plague will touch you when I strike Egypt. This is a day you are to commemorate; for the generations to come you shall celebrate it as a festival to the LORD—a lasting ordinance (Exod. 12: 11-14).

signified His blood must be shed (see Lev. 4:35); His hands and His feet were to be pierced (see Ps. 22:16); He was to be wounded and tormented (see Isa. 53:5); His ears were to be filled with revilings (see Ps. 22:6-8); His clothing would to whomever won the roll of dice ("cast lots," Ps. 22:18); and He was to drink vinegar (see Ps. 69:21). All of these incidents at the Messiah's death had been foretold in Jewish prophecy. But this was not the whole redemption story.

Jesus was put in Joseph's tomb, and on the third day He arose, as He had said He would. This was the supreme test of His kingship. People thought that He was dead and that His kingdom had failed. By the act of His resurrection, Christ assured His disciples that the King still lived and that one day He would come back to establish His kingdom on Earth.

The ascension of Jesus is not recorded in Matthew. The curtain falls with the Messiah still on Earth, for it is on Earth that the Son of David is yet to reign in glory. The last time the Jews

saw Christ, He was on the
Mount of Olives. The next time
they see Him He will again be on
the Mount of Olives (see Zech.
14:4; Acts 1:11-12).

A Worldwide Commission

Jesus announced His intentions,
and with this announcement a
crisis hour was struck in history.
The climax is His great commission to His followers:

> ***New Testament Fulfillment***
>
> *Take and eat; this is my
> body. . . . Drink from it, all of
> you. This is my blood of the
> covenant, which is poured out for
> many for the forgiveness of sins
> (Matt. 26:26-28).*
>
> *For Christ, our Passover lamb,
> has been sacrificed (1 Cor. 5:7).*

All authority in heaven and
on earth has been given to
me. Therefore go and make
disciples of all nations, bap-
tizing them in the name of the Father and of the Son
and of the Holy Spirit, and teaching them to obey
everything I have commanded you. And surely I am
with you always, to the very end of the age (Matt.
28:18-20).

On what mission were they sent? To overrun the world with
armies and make people submit under the sword? No, they
were commissioned to "make disciples of all nations."

The mountaintop of His ascension is where His disciples
started forth on this mission, radiating from that center. Christ's
followers today, the modern disciples, will go on until they have
reached the rim of the world. Christian faith is no national or

racial religion. It knows no bounds of mountain or sea. It envelops the entire globe.

STUDY GUIDE

Before you tackle these questions, please spend some time reading the Gospel of Matthew in the Bible.

Nothing is more clear in the Gospel of Matthew than the facts that Matthew was Jewish; he was writing primarily within a Jewish context and community; and Jewish people were his intended audience. Matthew wrote his Gospel to persuade Jewish people that Jesus was the Messiah who was promised in the Hebrew Bible (i.e., the Old Testament—the Jewish Scriptures).

COMING OF THE KING (MATTHEW 1–2)

1. How would the following Scripture passages have connected with Matthew's Jewish readers?

 • Matthew 1:1, which states: "A record of the *genealogy* of Jesus *Christ* the *son of David*, the *son of Abraham* (emphasis added). (Hint: Regarding "genealogy," quickly scan 1 Chronicles 1–9 and think about how important ancestry and bloodlines were in Jewish culture. Regarding "son of David," see "Understanding the Gospels," study question 6. Regarding "son of Abraham," review Henrietta Mears's commentary under "Coming of the King [Matthew 1—2].")

- Matthew 1:18-23, which depicts the moral dilemma facing Joseph—betrothed to a pregnant Mary—given the Jewish religious, social and cultural norms of the time.

- Matthew 1:22-23; 2:5-6,14-15,17-18,23; 3:3,15 (and many other places in Matthew's Gospel), which fulfill the prophecy of events surrounding Jesus' purpose, deeds and career.

- Matthew 2:1, which states that "Jesus was born in Bethlehem in Judea, during the time of King Herod." (Hint: Compare to 2 Kings 18:13; 24:1; Ezra 4:6—passages in which God events important in Jewish history are anchored to secular history. How is God's participation in human history different from nebulous, vague views of God that portray Him as either so far out there that He's aloof from human affairs, or as "it" that is an abstract and impersonal source of all "vibrations"?)

- Matthew 6:24; 19:27; 22:37, which reveal the basic assumption that there is one true God who deserves all worship, as opposed to other religions and world-views that embrace many gods and spirits. (Compare with Deuteronomy 6:4-5 and Exodus 20:3.)

Finding Truth

Many people seek to create God in their own image and likeness.

Ignoring the historical and cultural context Jesus lived in, they miss the intended messages coming out of that context.

A classic example of this tendency occurred in the 1930s when many German "Christians" bought hook, line and sinker the Nazi Aryan indoctrination that made Jesus into a virtual non-Jew and denigrated everything Jewish.

2. Can you think of any contemporary examples of people who ignore Jesus' Jewishness and message, and mold Him into an expression of their own religion or worldview? (Hint: Jesus as an "ascended master"—Hinduism; or Jesus as a revolutionary Marxist.)

3. What can we do to let the true message of Jesus speak to us and not get garbled?

PROCLAMATION OF THE KINGDOM (MATTHEW 3—16:20)

Jesus' famous Sermon on the Mount (see Matt. 5—7) is universally regarded as the most profound encapsulation of moral teaching in the Bible. Let's dig a little deeper into this mountain of spiritual truth.

4. Read the Beatitudes (see Matt. 5:3-12) and reflect on the meaning of each one. How are you doing on your poverty of spirit (admitting a desperate need for spiritual help from God), your meekness (controlling your strength according to God's direction), your hunger and thirst for righteousness (as opposed to

desiring entertainment or making more money) and your identifying with Christ despite public mockery and insults?

5. Take a look at Matthew 5:21-22,27-29. Jesus moves morality from mere behavior to the motives and thoughts of the heart. What is Jesus trying to teach us?

6. Notice Jesus' teaching on forgiveness in Matthew 6:12,14-15. According to Jesus, if you hold grudges and are unwilling to forgive others, do you have any right to expect forgiveness from God?

7. Matthew 7:12 says, "So in everything, do to others what you would have them do to you, for this sums up the Law and the Prophets." How can we, who are so compromised from the very start, have any chance to enter Christ's kingdom? (Hint: Go back to the first Beatitude [see Matt. 5:3].)

8. An important aspect of Jesus' ethical teaching is found in Matthew 23:23. According to Jesus, *all* of Scripture is God's Word, and *all* will be fulfilled (see Matt. 5:17-18); therefore, there are such things as moral absolutes. Yet here Jesus clearly acknowledges that *some* matters of the Law are *weightier* than others. What are these weightier matters?

Witnessing Miracles

Jesus' proclamation of God's kingdom was accompanied by

miracles; and we have plenty of them in Matthew 8—9.

9. What do you notice about the crowd's reactions to Jesus' miracles? Why would some people be apprehensive or angered by what Jesus did?

10. How would Jesus' miracles enhance His proclamation of the kingdom of God being "at hand" (see Matt. 4:17, *KJV*)?

Identifying with Christ

One of the most beautiful things about the Gospels is how they invite us into a discipleship relationship with Jesus, just like Jesus' 12 disciples had.

11. What hope do you take from the fact that the disciples Jesus chose were not the high and mighty ones in society?

12. Reread Matthew 10:32-33. According to Jesus, how important is it for Christians to publicly identify themselves with Christ? Why do you think this identification is so important to Jesus?

REJECTION OF THE KING (MATTHEW 16:21—20)

The previous question leads directly to what Henrietta Mears calls "Life's Most Important Question" and "Life's Most Important Answer."

13. What have you done personally with Jesus Christ? "Have you," as Mears asks, "put Christ on the throne of your life?" What would it mean to you if you took this step?

14. What does "become a Christian" mean? Is becoming a Christian just a matter of raising your hand at an evangelistic meeting? Or is it a matter of Christ profoundly altering you? Can Jesus take up residence in your life and not make a difference in you?

THE FUTURE OF THE KINGDOM (24—25)

15. Matthew's description of Jesus' sufferings for us on the cross, as anticipated by Old Testament stories and symbols, is discussed in the first paragraph under "The Great Price of Redemption." Look up the passages mentioned and reflect on what Jesus did for you, personally.

16. Matthew portrays Jesus not just as the promised Jewish Messiah but also as the Savior of the world. Turn to Matthew 28:18-20. Here, the resurrected Christ gives His disciples the Great Commission. Why is each phrase of the Great Commission significant?

   • Jesus first says, "All authority in heaven and on earth has been given to me" (v. 18). What type of person would say this kind of thing if it were not true? Do you think it is true? What kind of a person do you think Jesus is?

- Jesus then says, "Therefore go and make disciples of all nations . . . teaching them to obey everything I have commanded you" (vv. 19-20). The phrase "all nations" means "all the ethnic groups of the world." According to this passage, did Jesus want any ethnic groups to be left to themselves so that they could remain as they are and practice whatever religion they saw fit?

- Jesus adds, "Baptizing them in the name of the Father and of the Son and of the Holy Spirit" (v. 19). This baptismal formula in the name of the Trinity acknowledges God as the great Three-in-One. Have you been baptized in the name of the Father and of the Son and of the Holy Spirit?

- Jesus concludes, "And surely I am with you always, to the very end of the age" (v. 20). This promise is amazing. Jesus says that He will personally be with each and every one of His followers "always." Never again do we have to feel alone, because Jesus is here. Since Jesus really is in the *here and now*, what would you like to say to Him? Say it silently or say it out loud; it doesn't matter. But say something from your heart.

Note

1. *Merriam-Webster's Collegiate Dictionary*, 10th ed., s.v. "genealogy."

CHAPTER 3

UNDERSTANDING mark

Mark Portrays Jesus Christ, the Servant of God

John, whose surname was Mark, was the writer of the Gospel of Mark (see Acts 12:12,25). He was the son of Mary and cousin of Barnabas (see Col. 4:10) and likely was a native of Jerusalem. He accompanied Paul and Barnabas to Antioch (see Acts 12:25; 13:5) and was the cause of a serious disagreement between them (see Acts 15:36-40). Then he left them, probably on account of hardships (see Acts 13:13). Finally, he became a great help to Paul (see Col. 4:10-11; 2 Tim. 4:11). It is believed that the disciples met in the Upper Room of Mark's mother's house in Jerusalem. Peter was the means of Mark's conversion, and Peter affectionately speaks of Mark as "my son" (1 Pet. 5:13), so Peter's teaching influenced this Gospel.

If we turn to Mark 10:45, we can quite easily determine Mark's goal in writing his Gospel:

> For even the Son of Man did not come to be served, but
> to serve, and to give his life as a ransom for many.

Unlike Matthew, Mark was not trying to prove certain statements and prophecies concerning Jesus. His only objective in writing was to tell clearly certain facts about Jesus—His deeds more than His words. He proved that Jesus is the Son of God—not by declaring how He came to Earth, but by showing what He accomplished during His brief career on Earth and how His coming changed the world.

There is a general agreement that Mark's Gospel was written for a Roman audience. The Roman culture differed in many ways from the Jewish culture. The Romans highly valued strong common sense. Their religion was practical. They had no interest in tracing beliefs back to the past. Legal genealogies and fulfillments of prophecy left them cold. Arguing fine points of Scripture held no interest for them. They might have said, "I know nothing of your Scriptures and care nothing for your peculiar notions, but I should be glad to hear a plain story of the life this man Jesus lived. Tell me what He did. Let me see Him just as He was."

Mark differs widely from Matthew in both character and scope. Mark's Gospel is the shortest of them all. The book of Matthew has 28 chapters, abounds in parables and portrays Christ as the Son of David with kingly dignity and authority (see Matt. 28:18). Mark has 16 chapters and gives four parables. Mark portrays Christ as the humble but perfect servant of Jehovah, whose angels minister to Him.

UNIQUE CHARACTERISTICS

The skill of an artist may lie in what he or she leaves out. An amateur crowds everything in. Omissions are evident in the Gospel of Mark. There is nothing about the virgin birth—no reference to His birth is made in the whole Gospel. This is significant. No one is interested in the pedigree of a servant.

There is no visit of wise men. A servant does not receive homage.

No account of Jesus as the boy in the Temple is given. In this practical age, as in the age of Jesus, people demand a Christ who can do things. They are not interested in Jesus the boy but Christ the man who is able and willing to accomplish today what He did of old.

Mark does not describe the Sermon on the Mount. Matthew devotes three chapters to this sermon, which sets forth the laws of the Kingdom and describes the character of its subjects. Mark presents Christ as a perfect workman; a servant has no kingdom and frames no laws.

Fewer quotations from the prophets are imparted in Mark than in Matthew. Mark quotes the Old Testament a dozen times whereas Matthew quotes it on nearly every page.

No divine titles are used. Jesus is never owned as King in Mark, except in derision. Matthew says, " 'They will call him Immanuel'—which means, 'God with us' " (1:23). Not so in Mark. Mark calls Him "teacher" (4:38; 5:35) or "Master" (*KJV*). Other evangelists call Him "Lord."

Matthew 8:25 says, "Lord, save us! We're going to drown!" while Mark 4:38 says, "Teacher, don't you care if we drown?"

There is no statement that His work was finished at His death. In John 19:30, Jesus said, "It is finished." This is not found in Mark. It is not for a servant to say when his work is done.

There is no introduction in Mark. The other Gospels have lengthy openings, but there is none in Mark. The opening verse says, "The beginning of the gospel about Jesus Christ." Mark adds "Son of God" to guard His divine glory. How different this is from Matthew, where we find the Gospel of the Kingdom.

The word "gospel" is used 12 times in Matthew, Mark, Luke and John together; eight of those times are in Mark. Yes, the servant is to bear good news!

The Greek word *eutheos*, which means "immediately," "at once," "as soon as" and "without delay" is found no fewer than 40 times in Mark's Gospel. This is a servant's word.

In the *King James Version*, 12 out of 16 chapters in Mark open with the little word "and." Jesus' service was one complete, perfect whole, with no pauses or breaks in it. His service was continuous. We slacken, but our Lord does not.

As we mentioned earlier, Mark's Gospel is the shortest of the four Gospels. Very little is found here that is not found in the others. It moves with precision.

Matthew records 14 parables. Mark records only four—the sower, the seed growing secretly (peculiar to Mark), the mustard seed and the wicked husbandmen. Not only do you find omission in number, but you also find omission in type. There is nothing about the householder, the marriage of the king's son or the talents.

Miracles have a leading place in Mark, as parables have in Matthew. A servant works; a king speaks. Mark describes more of Jesus' miracles than parables. In fact, he describes 20 miracles in detail.

THE SERVANT PREPARED (MARK 1:1-13)

The Gospel of Mark skips over the first 30 years of Jesus' life, but these years were necessary for His human preparation for His life's work. His sympathy with daily toil grew. He wrestled, like Jacob, with life's problems. He fought many battles in the arena of His heart. He meditated upon the needs of His nation until His heart burned within Him.

Old Testament Promise and New Testament Fulfillment

A voice of one calling: "In the desert prepare the way for the LORD; make straight in the wilderness a highway for our God" (Isa. 40:3).

And this was his [John the Baptist] message: "After me will come one more powerful than I, the thongs of whose sandals I am not worthy to stoop down and untie. I baptize you with water, but he will baptize you with the Holy Spirit" (Mark 1:7-8).

Preparation in life is needed. Jesus' life illustrated this. The foundations of the lighthouse are necessary, though unseen beneath the surface. The coral colony builds the foundations for an island and its tropical growth. The plant sends its roots into the dark soil before it can bring forth the flower and leaf. Look at the 40 years Moses spent in the desert before he entered upon his great work; the long period of Elijah's youth before he appeared before King Ahab; the youth of Amos spent on a farm; John the Baptist's 30 years of training. So with Jesus! He spent 30 years in obscurity in Nazareth before He appeared for His three years of public ministry. Getting ready for our life's work is of tremendous importance. Don't chafe if Christ uses time in preparing you for life.

Preparation by John the Forerunner

This Gospel begins with John the Baptist preparing for the coming of the Messiah. John's coming was fulfilled a messianic prophecy: "I will send my messenger ahead of you, who will prepare your way" (Mark 1:2). This quotation refers to Malachi 3:1 and Isaiah 40:3. Isaiah says the messenger is known simply as "a voice":

> A voice of one calling: "In the desert prepare the way for the LORD; make straight in the wilderness a highway for our God" (Isa. 40:3).

It is this voice that is to be the herald of Jesus Christ.

We see this strange man who appears on the scene in an almost sensational way: "John wore clothing made of camel's hair, with a leather belt around his waist, and he ate locusts and wild honey" (Mark 1:6).

There is a lesson here for us. God does not always choose the kind of person we would select. He often picks "the foolish things of the world to shame the wise . . . the weak things of the world to shame the strong" (1 Cor. 1:27). No doubt, if we were to select a herald for Christ, we would choose someone of high birth, who has been university trained and who enjoys a wide reputation. This person would have to be eloquent and a fearless champion of great causes. Not so with God. Of humble birth, unknown and dressed like a desert hermit, John the Baptist was approved of God (see Matt. 11:11).

As noted in the chapter on Matthew, John's message was as startling as his appearance. He went ahead of his monarch as any Roman officer would go ahead of his, demanding that the road be repaired and the highway reconstructed: "Prepare the way for the Lord, make straight paths for him" (Mark 1:3). A true revival is always a revival of righteousness.

Preparation by Baptism

John and Jesus met one day. John recognized immediately that this man was not a subject for the baptism of repentance. Christ's purity and majesty smote John's heart with a sense of his own unworthiness. He knew he had encountered the Son of God. John hesitated, and said, "I need to be baptized by you, and do you come to me?" (Matt. 3:14).

Jesus was baptized by John in obedience to an appointed ordinance: "Let it be so now; it is proper for us to do this to fulfill all righteousness" (Matt. 3:15). Jesus set a seal of approval on John's message and work, and He acknowledged him as the true forerunner of Christ. The baptism by John was ordained of God and therefore was binding on all those who acknowledged God and meant to keep His commandments.

Christ was the standard and example of righteousness. He would fulfill every duty He required of others (see 1 Cor. 10:13).

Preparation by Receiving the Holy Spirit

"As Jesus was coming up out of the water, he saw heaven being torn open and the Spirit descending on him like a dove" (Mark 1:10). The Spirit descended not only in the manner of a dove but also in the bodily shape of a dove (see Luke 3:22). This was a symbol, although the coming of the Spirit Himself was a reality. Every event in Jesus' life had significance. In any service for God, the Spirit always prepares the life by giving power and equipment. He is God's great agent for spiritual warfare.

Old Testament Prophecy and New Testament Fulfillment

I will proclaim the decree of the LORD: He said to me, "You are my Son; today I have become your Father. Ask of me, and I will make the nations your inheritance, the ends of the earth your possession" (Ps. 2:7-8).

Then a cloud appeared and enveloped them, and a voice came from the cloud: "This is my Son, whom I love. Listen to him!" (Mark 9:7).

Because Jesus went down into the baptismal water of obedience to God, He came up under an opened sky with the Holy Spirit descending upon Him, and the voice of His Father declaring Him to be His beloved Son was heard.

Jesus came up out of that water a new man into a new world. His relationship to His Father and His mission were proclaimed.

Preparation by a Divine Call

"A voice came from heaven" (Mark 1:11). God endorsed Jesus and His mission and showed to the Jewish nation that Jesus was the Messiah:

God anointed Jesus of Nazareth with the Holy Spirit and power, and how he went around doing good and healing all who were under the power of the devil, because God was with him (Acts 10:38).

This has been called Mark's Gospel in a nutshell. Later we hear this same voice at Jesus' transfiguration: "This is my Son, whom I love. Listen to him!" (Mark 9:7).

Preparation by Testing

Baptism and temptation are crowded together here. The voice from heaven had barely died away when a whisper from hell was heard. Out of the baptismal benediction of the Father, Jesus stepped into a desperate struggle with the devil.

Mark says, "At once the Spirit sent him out into the desert" (1:12), which shows how quickly the Spirit moves. "At once" indicates continuity, showing that temptation was as much a part of the servant's preparation for His work as was His baptism. (Suffering and trial are as much God's plan as are thrills and triumphs.) Jesus was led to be tempted. It was no accident or evil fate but a divine appointment. Temptation has its place in this world. We would never develop without it. There is nothing wrong in being tempted. The wrong begins when we begin to consent to it. Further, we are not to run into temptation of our own accord—Jesus did not go of Himself but was led of the Spirit. We will find that the path of duty often takes us through temptations, but we need not succumb to them:

> No temptation has seized you except what is common to man. And God is faithful; he will not let you be tempted beyond what you can bear. But when you are tempted, he will also provide a way out so that you can stand up under it (1 Cor. 10:13).

He always makes a way of escape!

THE SERVANT WORKING
(MARK 1:14—8:30)

There is a continuous, unbroken service of the servant record-ed in this Gospel. Mark provides many examples of what Jesus did and said. Jesus taught people; they were in darkness. He cheered people; they were without hope. He healed people; they were sick and suffering. He freed people; they were under the power of Satan. He pardoned and cleansed people; they were sinful.

We see Jesus preaching by the seashore and selecting four fishermen to become His first disciples to learn under His guidance how to become "fishers of men" (Mark 1:17). They were to turn all the practical knowledge and skill they exercised in the art of catching fish into the work of catching men and women for Christ. Who was called in Mark 1:16-20? What disciple was called in Mark 2?

How was Christ's call received? "At once they left their nets and followed him" (Mark 1:18). It is interesting to note that Jesus never called any person from idleness. He called busy and successful people to follow Him.

Everyone can turn a business into a channel of service for Christ. Too often there is lost time between our call and our coming; our doing lags far behind our duty.

Jesus is introduced at once as anointed with power and as fully engaged in His work. You will find no long discourses in Mark, but you will find many mighty deeds. Demons were cast out (see 1:21-28); a fever banished (see 1:29-31); diseases healed (see 1:32-34); lepers made whole (see 1:40-45); a paralytic man made to walk (see 2:1-12); a withered hand cured (see 3:1-5); mul-titudes healed (see 3:7-12); a storm at sea quelled (see 4:35-41);

a maniac's mind restored (see 5:1-15); a woman's blood hemorrhage stopped (see 5:21-34); Jairus's daughter brought back to life (see 5:35-43); five thousand people fed (see 6:32-44); the sea made into His sidewalk (see 6:45-51); all who touched Him made whole (see 6:53-56); the deaf and dumb heard and spoke (see 7:31-37); four thousand people fed (see 8:1-9); and a blind man healed (see 8:22-26).

The action is rapid; events appear to be happening before our eyes. Mark's descriptions are abrupt and outspoken, but he preserves many things for us that otherwise would have been lost. It is only in the Gospel of Mark that we are told Jesus was a carpenter (see Mark 6:3).

Mark tells us that He "took [one] by the hand" (1:31) and little children "in his arms" (10:16). Mark tells us that Jesus was "grieved" (14:34, NASB), that He "sighed" (8:12) and that He "wondered" (6:6, NASB). He "loved" (10:21), and He was angry (see 3:5). He was touched with the feelings of our infirmities (see 5:31).

The Servant Performs Miracles

Let's spend the Sabbath with Jesus (see Mark 1:21-34)—going with Him to synagogue, listening to His preaching, watching Him when interrupted by a maniac, witnessing Him cast out the unclean spirit and noticing healing as a powerful aid to His teaching. After the service, let's go with Him to Peter's house and see Him heal Peter's mother-in-law of a severe fever, and then let us spend the Sabbath afternoon in quiet rest and friendly conversation. Toward evening we'll look out in the beautiful twilight and see men and women coming toward the house, bringing great numbers of people who are sick with every kind of disease. Let us watch as Jesus lays His tender hands upon them and heals them. The lame jump from their stretchers and leap for joy; the blind open their eyes and see their healer; lines of suffering turn to expressions of unbelievable happiness as people are delivered from their painful diseases.

Mark records a wonderful statement concerning the Sabbath: "The Sabbath was made for man, not man for the Sabbath" (2:27). This great saying of Jesus is the central principle of Sabbath observance. The Sabbath was not made to annoy humankind, to confine us or to impoverish us; it was created to enrich and bless us! Let's try spending one Lord's day as Jesus did—the Lord will be pleased.

Christ answers the question of Sabbath with a practical illustration. His point is that whatever deed is really helpful to people is proper for the Sabbath and is in perfect harmony with God's design of the day. He illustrates this truth with a miracle of healing (see Mark 3:1-5). Seven of Jesus' recorded miracles are performed on the Sabbath.

The miracles of Jesus are also proof of His mission from God. They showed that He is the promised redeemer and King—the One we all need. Because Jesus is God, miracles are as natural to Him as acts of will are to us. Through His miracles, Jesus inspires faith.

The servant is always found working: "As long as it is day, we must do the work of him who sent me. Night is coming, when no one can work" (John 9:4). As we read this memorandum of the full days of our Lord's ministry, how empty our own lives seem in comparison!

The Servant Prays

On the morning following the great Sabbath day of preaching and healing, He arose very early and went out of the city to a lonely place and prayed (see Mark 1:35). His work was growing rapidly, and Jesus needed heavenly communion. The seeming answer was a larger work—the entrance upon His first Galilean tour of healing and preaching (see vv. 37-39). Only one healing event of this tour, which lasted several days, is recorded—that of a leper whose disease was incurable (see vv. 40-45).

If the Son of God needed to pray before He undertook His work, how much more should we pray? Perhaps if we lack success in life, it is because we fail at this task. We have not because we ask not (see Jas. 4:2).

The Servant Forgives Sin

"A few days later . . . the people heard that he had come home" (Mark 2:1). It is remarkable how rapidly news spread during the Bible times when there were no television, telephones, radios or computers. In another part of the city a paralytic man heard of this new prophet and His gospel of healing. His four friends brought him into the presence of the teacher. We find in this healing the test and proof of Jesus' power, not only as a physician of the body, but also as a healer of the soul: "Who can forgive sins but God alone?" (v. 7). Sins are against God and, therefore, He only can forgive. Jesus said:

> "But that you may know that the Son of Man has authority on earth to forgive sins . . . ." He said to the paralytic, "I tell you, get up, take your mat and go home" (vv. 10-11).

In this miracle, God endorsed Jesus' claim to be the Messiah. The man arose, took up his bed and went forth before them all, a living witness to Jesus' power over sin—a visible illustration of the work Jesus came to do. Jesus came to give His life as a ransom for many so that He might forgive people their sins (see Mark 10:45). "All have sinned" (Rom. 3:23), and all need a Savior.

The Servant Chooses the Twelve, Teaches Parables and Performs More Miracles

We find the account of Jesus choosing the 12 apostles in Mark 3:13-19. Notice verse 14. It tells that Jesus chose these men so "that they might be with him." Let's mark it in our Bibles. This is what Jesus wants of His disciples today—that we will take time to be in His presence and commune with Him. In John 15:15, He says, "I no longer call you servants. . . . I have called you friends."

As we turn to Mark 4, notice once again that the opening word is "and" (*KJV*): "And he began again to teach." The chapter continues with the parable of the sower, which explains the hindrances to the Gospel that dwell in the hearts of the hearers (see vv. 3-20).

Everyone should master these parables of the Kingdom in

Mark 4. They were a special teaching instrument of Christ. Jesus used this method of instruction because of the growing hostility toward Him and His message. He was surrounded by enemies who tried to trip Him over His words, but no one could object to a simple story. Besides, stories are remembered by the dullest of hearers.

A parable is an analogythat illustrates using a likeness between heavenly and earthly things. "Parable" comes from the Greek word meaning "beside" and "to throw." A parable, then, is a form of teaching in which one thing is thrown beside another to make a comparison.

Besides the parable of the sower, Mark recorded other parables of our Lord:

- The parable of the lamp (see vv. 21-25)
- The parable of the sprouting seed (see vv. 26-29)
- The parable of the mustard seed (see vv. 30-34)

After interpreting the parables, Jesus took a ship to escape the crowd. On the way, as the weary teacher fell asleep, a violent storm arose on the Sea of Galilee. About to perish, the frantic disciples awoke Jesus. At a word from His lips, the sea became calm. He even had power over the elements (see vv. 35-41).

Mark 5 also begins with "and" (KJV). Jesus is still working. What does He do now? Read parallel accounts in Matthew 8:28-34 and Luke 8:26-39. Compare this miracle with other recorded cures of demoniacs in Matthew 9:32-33; 17:14-18; Mark 1:23-26 and Luke 9:38-42.

The miracle recorded in Mark 5, like all others, tested the character of people. It caught them off guard and disclosed their true natures. Notice the contrast in the way people received the work of Christ.

Some shunned the Savior. "Those tending the pigs ran off. . . . and they were afraid" (vv. 14-15) and "began to plead with Jesus to leave their region" (v. 17). There were other herds of swine no doubt, and they feared the loss of them. What a true picture of the attitude of many of us toward Christ! We have some gainful business we do not want to give up. We have some sin that lies close to our hearts. For these reasons we thrust Christ away.

Some sought the Savior. The healed man begged Him, not to depart out of his boat, but "to go with him" (v. 18). People do the same thing today. They either ask Jesus to depart because they want to keep their sin, or they ask that He might remain with them because they want to lose their sin. Do we want to keep or lose our sin?

"And" starts another episode in Jesus' miracles (v. 21, *KJV*). After healing the demoniac, Jesus returned to Capernaum. He healed a woman long sick; and "while Jesus was still speaking" (v. 35), He was called upon to raise a child already lying in death, Jairus's daughter.

Then Jesus started out on a third preaching tour of Galilee (see Mark 6). He sent the 12 disciples, two by two, on independent missions (see vv. 7-13). Matthew 10 records the instructions they received. As they preached, Herod heard them and we read of his uneasy conscience, thinking that the man he had murdered was back to haunt him (see vv. 14-29).

How much we recklessly give away for passing pleasures. For a glass of wine, a moment of passion, a little more money, a position of empty honor, we give away our souls, health, home, friendships, peace, happiness and eternal life. Like Esau, we sell our birthright for a bowl of food (see Gen. 25:29-34). Like Judas, we sell our Savior for 30 pieces of silver (see Matt. 26:14-16).

After the apostles were trained, Jesus sent them on an extensive missionary tour to the villages of Galilee (see Mark 6:12-13). On returning they "gathered around Jesus" (v. 30), probably at their regular rendezvous, Capernaum. They gave reports about their sermons, the number of conversions and the miracles that were wrought. No Christian work can be carried on long without frequent talks with Christ. We need His sympathy, approval, guidance and strength.

We must steadily move forward if we want to follow this mighty servant—this workman of God. Jesus went to a desert to rest awhile, but the multitudes followed Him (see vv. 31-32). Feeding the five thousand followed without an interval (see vv. 32-44). This was one of the most important miracles, as it is the only one of the 35 miracles recorded by all four Gospel writers. Let's review it carefully and notice Jesus served in an orderly way.

What miracles are next (see vv. 45-56)? What does Jesus do and say in Mark 7; 8:1-9,22-26?

Peter's confession of faith should be mastered by everyone (see Mark 8:29). Jesus did not tell His disciples who He was. He waited until they told Him. When He asked, "Who do you say I am?" (v. 29), the climax of His ministry was reached. He was testing the aim of all His training of the chosen twelve. Peter's answer gave Him the assurance that His goal had been attained.

What did the Pharisees think of Jesus? They had already agreed to put Him to death.

What did the multitudes think of Him? Already they were deserting Him.

*Old Testament Promise and
New Testament Fulfillment*

*Rejoice greatly, O Daughter of
Zion! Shout, Daughter of
Jerusalem! See, your king comes
to you, righteous and having salvation, gentle and riding on a
donkey, on a colt, the foal of a
donkey (Zech. 9:9).*

*When they brought the colt to
Jesus and threw their cloaks over
it, he sat on it. Those who went
ahead and those who followed
shouted, "Hosanna!" "Blessed is
he who comes in the name of the
Lord!" (Mark 11:7,9).*

What did the disciples think
of Him? Peter gave the answer.

What do we think of Christ?

THE SERVANT REJECTED (MARK 8:31—15)

Even before Mark established
Christ's direct claim to be King
of the Kingdom, he revealed the
way the King was to be received.
His was a pathway of suffering
and rejection. Jesus said, "The
Son of Man must suffer many
things" (Mark 8:31). The evangelist wrote it down in plain
language—Jesus was to be rejected by the rulers of Israel and
killed, only to rise again on the
third day:

- Jesus told His disciples that He was to be rejected by
  the elders, chief priests and scribes (see Mark 8:31).
- He was to be delivered by treachery (see Mark 9:31).
- He was to be put to death by the Romans (see Mark
  10:32-45).
- He was to rise again on the third day (see Mark 9:31).
- Jesus, nevertheless, claimed the Kingdom by pre-
  senting Himself at Jerusalem as the heir of David,

according to the prophecy of Zechariah 9:9 (see Matt. 21:1-5; Mark 11:1-11).

How did the people accept this King? At first they welcomed Him because they hoped He might deliver them from the yoke of Rome and free them from the poverty they were enduring. But when He entered the Temple and showed that His mission was a spiritual one, He was hated by the religious leaders with a satanic hatred that led to the plot to put Him to death (see Mark 14:1).

The World's Greatest Sin

The greatest sin of this age, as of every age, is the rejection of Jesus Christ. Remember that everyone who has heard the gospel must either accept the Lord as Savior or trample Him underfoot. The people of Jesus' day made their choice and we must make ours.

This wonderful presence that shines forth in the Gospels, this vision of God in the flesh—do you to look and then pass on as though you had but seen a work of art? This voice that sounds throughout the centuries—do you listen as though it were just the voice of a gifted orator? What is Jesus to you? A name? Or your master?

Old Testament Promise and New Testament Fulfillment

For my house will be called a house of prayer for all nations (Isa. 56:7).

On reaching Jerusalem, Jesus entered the temple area and began driving out those who were buying and selling there. And as he taught them, he said, "Is it not written: 'My house will be called a house of prayer for all nations?' But you have made it 'a den of robbers'" (Mark 11:15,17).

The World's Rejection

After Christ's public ministry, described in Mark 10:46—11:26, we read of His last conflict with the Jewish authorities and of His triumph over the leaders (see Mark 11:27—12:44).

Jesus sought to persuade the Jews to receive Him as the Messiah (see Mark 11:15—12:44). It was a busy Tuesday, occupied from morning until night in one great and powerful effort to induce the Jewish nation to acknowledge Him and thus become that glorious nation, blessing the world, for which it had been set apart.

In the beautiful Temple courts, the simple Galilean met the religious authorities arrayed in all the pomp of their official regalia. There was a sharp and prolonged controversy on several puzzling questions.

The scribes and chief priests asked Jesus, "By what authority are you doing these things? And who gave you authority to do this?" (Mark 11:28).

The Pharisees and Herodians tried to catch Jesus in His words by asking, "Is it right to pay taxes to Caesar or not?" (Mark 12:14).

The Sadducees, who said there was no resurrection, asked Him, "At the resurrection whose wife will she be, since the seven were married to her?" (v. 23).

The scribes asked Him, "Of all the commandments, which is the most important?" (v. 28).

After Jesus answered them all, "from then on no one dared ask him any more questions" (v. 34).

It would seem that He could not escape treason to the Roman government in answering them, but He emerged unscathed. Hour by hour Jesus met the attack.

All the way through, the perfect servant of God was dogged by His enemies. Jesus silenced His enemies, but their hearts would not yield. Then He exposed all of their hypocritical practices in words that fell like bombs. He tried to break through their walls of prejudice and cause them to repent before it was too late, but all seemed to be in vain.

Before He went to the cross, Jesus revealed the future to His troubled disciples in the discourse on the Mount of Olives (see Mark 13). He told them of the end of this age and of the great tribulation, and climaxed it with the promise of His return in power and glory.

Old Testament Promise and New Testament Fulfillment

We all, like sheep, have gone astray, each of us has turned to his own way; and the LORD has laid on him the iniquity of us all (Isa. 53:6).

For Christ died for sins once for all, the righteous for the unrighteous, to bring you to God. He was put to death in the body but made alive by the Spirit (1 Pet. 3:18).

The plotting of the chief priests—how they might take Him by craft and put Him to death (see v. 1)—and the anointing of His body in preparation for burial (see v. 8) open Mark 14. Then the ever sad story of His betrayal at the hand of His own disciple (see vv. 10-11), the celebration of the Passover and the institution of the Lord's Supper are crowded into 25 short verses. Adding insult to injury, we read of Peter's denial of Jesus (see vv. 26-31,66-71).

Isaiah's great message is that the Son of God shall become the servant of God in order that He might die to redeem the world. Mark records how the sufferings of Jesus in Gethsemane (see Mark 14:32-41) and on Calvary (see Mark 15:21-37) fulfilled the prophecies of Isaiah (see Isa. 53).

Jesus was sold for 30 pieces of silver—the price of a slave. He was executed as only slaves were. Yes, Christ was the suffering servant and died for us! He bore our sins in His own body on the tree.

No reference is made by Mark that in the garden Jesus had the right to summon 12 legions of angels if He so willed (see Matt. 26:53). No promise of the Kingdom is given to the dying thief on the cross (see Luke 23:40-43). These claims are made by a King in Matthew, but they are not mentioned by a servant in Mark.

THE SERVANT EXALTED (MARK 16)

After the servant gave His life as a ransom for many (see Mark 10:45), He arose from the dead (see Mark 16:6). We read again the Great Commission (see vv. 15-18), which also is recorded in Matthew 28:19-20. Compare the two. In Mark we do not hear a King say, "All authority in heaven and on earth has been given to me," as we do in Matthew. In Mark, we see in Jesus' words that His disciples are to take His place; and He will serve in and through them. He is yet the worker, though risen (see v. 20). The command rings with urgency of purpose—not a corner of the world is to be left unvisited, not a soul to be left out!

Finally, the servant of Jehovah is received into heaven to sit at the right hand of God (see Ps. 110:1; Mark 16:19). He who had taken upon Himself the form of a servant is now highly exalted (see Phil. 2:7-9). He is in the place of power, ever making intercession for us. He is our advocate.

Christ is with us. The servant is always working in us and through us. We are laborers together with Him (see 1 Cor. 3:9). He is still working with us (see Mark 16:20). Let us, being redeemed, follow Jesus' pattern and also go forth to serve!

Therefore, my dear brothers, stand firm. Let nothing move you. Always give yourselves fully to the work of the Lord, because you know that your labor in the Lord is not in vain (1 Cor. 15:58).

Old Testament Promise and New Testament Fulfillment

The LORD says to my Lord: "Sit at my right hand until I make your enemies a footstool for your feet" (Ps. 110:1).

After the Lord Jesus had spoken to them, he was taken up into heaven and he sat at the right hand of God (Mark 16:19).

STUDY GUIDE

Whereas Matthew's Gospel was crafted particularly for a Jewish audience, Mark's Gospel was designed to reach the Romans, or people culturally dominated by Roman culture and thinking. The Romans were non-Jews—aware of Jewish culture and religion, and had dealings with Jewish people, but not necessarily familiar with all things Jewish. Mark, whose message is just as universal as Matthew's (see Matt. 28:18-20),

makes a special effort to make the gospel of Jesus understand-
able to the Romans. Let's put this into context.

1. The Romans promoted a certain amount of tolerance
   for religions, even though they also promoted emperor
   worship and supremacy of the Roman state. Read
   Mark 1:1,15. Why would Mark's mention of Jesus as
   the Son of God and the kingdom of God as being "at
   hand" have gotten the attention of Roman readers?

2. The Romans valued *pietas* (duty), *gravitas* (seriousness
   of purpose) and *dignitas* (a sense of personal worth).
   Quickly review the section headings in Mark 1, starting with the heading above verse 21. How would chapter 1 have meshed with Roman sensibilities?

3. The Romans thought they were above what they per-
   ceived as narrow-mindedness. Read Mark 2:23—3:6,
   which describes Jesus' treatment of the Sabbath. What
   principles did Jesus use to supercede the Pharisee's
   idea of keeping the Sabbath? What reactions might a
   Roman reader have had to this story?

4. The Romans would likely have been baffled by the
   intricacies of Jewish traditions about what was reli-
   giously clean and unclean. Read Mark 7:1-23. What
   does Mark say to help his Roman readers understand
   the issues at stake? How does this section, especially
   starting with verse 14, speak universally to all people,
   not just the Romans? (Hint: See verses 3-4,19.)

Read again these other passages, which Mark wrote to help his readers who are unfamiliar with Jewish language and customs: 3:17; 5:41; 7:34; 15:16,22,34,42.

5. Among the Romans were many God fearers (see Acts 10:2). These were people fed up with the mythologies and superstitions of polytheistic religion and were attracted to the purity of monotheism as taught in Judaism. They might have visited a synagogue, but they weren't ready to convert to Judaism. What might a typical God-fearer have thought of Mark 12:28-34?

THE LORD AS KING AND SERVANT

While a major theme of Matthew's Gospel is the kingdom of God, with Jesus as the messianic King, Mark's Gospel abundantly emphasizes Jesus as the servant of God.

6. Think about kings, queens and monarchies in two opposing ways: (1) what attracts us; and (2) what repels us?

7. Now think through Jesus' career on Earth as presented by Matthew and Mark. How is Jesus like a king; and how does He break with kingly stereotypes? (Hint: Mears provides a lot of examples.)

THE SERVANT PREPARED (MARK 1:1-13)

Henrietta Mears does something very interesting in the next two sections. She likens Jesus' human life to ours.

8. Reflecting on how God prepared Jesus for His life's work, Mears says, "Preparation in life is needed. . . . Getting ready for our life's work is of tremendous importance. Don't chafe if Christ uses time in preparing you for life." How can you bring Christ into your preparation for your life's work today?

9. Reflecting on the oddness of John the Baptist, Mears says, "There is a lesson here for us. God does not always choose the kind of person we would select. He often picks 'the foolish things of the world to shame the wise . . . the weak things of the world to shame the strong' (1 Cor. 1:27)." How often have you written yourself off as someone too odd for God to use significantly? How often have you written others off that way? Can you repent of that attitude right now and again put your life in His hands, at His disposal? Can you ask Him to see the potential in others, even if you might not choose them?

10. Reflecting on John's message of repentance, Mears says, "A true revival is always a revival of righteousness." Revivals are a mixture of human and divine elements. A revival is true when people are awakened to God's reality through Christ, and their lives are transformed by that experience. A false revival is when peo-

ple go through the motions but aren't really changed. For Christians who really want to walk with Christ, is there ever a time when revival ought to end?

11. Reflecting on the temptation of Christ, Henrietta Mears says, "Suffering and trial are as much God's plan as are thrills and triumphs." Let that sink in a while. It's not often preached as straight as that, but it's as true for Jesus as it is for you. Pray this thought back to the Lord.

12. Henrietta Mears also says some remarkable things based upon the Scriptures:

- "Jesus was led to be tempted. It was no accident or evil fate but a divine appointment."
- "Temptation has its place in this world. We would never develop without it."
- "There is nothing wrong in being tempted. The wrong begins when we begin to consent to it."
- "We will find that the path of duty often takes us through temptations."
- "He always makes a way of escape [from temptation]!"

Meditate on each of these thoughts, and apply each of them to your own life. Repent as needed. Then memorize and meditate on 1 Corinthians 10:13.

THE SERVANT WORKING
(MARK 1:14—8:30)

Henrietta Mears's discussion continues as she likens Jesus' human life to ours.

13. Reflecting on Jesus' calling of fishermen to follow Him and become "fishers of men," Mears says, "It is interesting to note that Jesus never called any person from idleness." This is vintage Henrietta Mears. She advocated the strenuous life and lived unabashedly for the Lord Jesus Christ. How are you fully engaged in the great gift of life?

14. Reflecting on the phrase "at once they left their nets and followed him" (Mark 1:18), Mears says, "Too often there is lost time between our call and our coming; our doing lags far behind our duty." In what ways have you tried to put God on hold rather than quickly obeying Him or following His lead in your life?

15. Reflecting on the fact that Jesus made time to get away from the crowds and pray alone with God, Mears says, "If the Son of God needed to pray before He undertook His work, how much more should we pray? Perhaps if we lack success in life, it is because we fail at this task. We have not because we ask not (see Jas. 4:2)." Are you taking each of your endeavors to God in prayer? When are you going to set up a regular, daily habit of bringing your concerns to God?

16. One passage that forever establishes Jesus' unique claim to deity is Mark 2:1-11. Jesus, the servant of God, heals the paralytic man, which proves His healing power and authority from God for spiritual healing from sin. The most disarming thing you can say to someone about your Christian faith is "Jesus died for sinners like me." Are you able to say this about yourself? Can you tell it to others?

17. Reflecting on Jesus' choice of the 12 apostles in Mark 3, Mears focuses on the phrase "that they might be with him" (v. 14). She says, "Let's mark it in our Bibles." Get your Bible out and do it now! The point of being a Christian is that we might be with Christ every moment of every day.

18. Reflecting on how Jesus gathered His followers together after their first missionary journey (see Mark 6:30), Mears says, "No Christian work can be carried on long without frequent talks with Christ. We need His sympathy, approval, guidance and strength." Do you see what Mark's Gospel is teaching us? As it was for the disciples, so it is for us. Take some time now to seek Jesus' sympathy, approval, guidance and strength. He's waiting for you right now.

THE SERVANT REJECTED (MARK 8:31—15)

In this section, Henrietta Mears continues to bring home the implications of Mark's Gospel. Reflecting on the plot that led to Jesus' death (see Mark 14:1), Mears reminds us that the message of Jesus is like a sword that divides: "The greatest sin of this age, as of every age, is the rejection of Jesus Christ. Remember that everyone who has heard the gospel must either accept the Lord as Savior or trample Him underfoot. The people of Jesus' day made their choice and the people of our day must make theirs."

19. Do you agree that the greatest sin is to reject Jesus Christ? Why or why not?

20. Henrietta Mears says, "The greatest sin of this age, as of every age, is the rejection of Jesus Christ." This might be a bit hyperbolic, since there were believers in God's true revelation before Jesus was born. Can you make sense of how believers in God could have believed in Jesus before Jesus was born? (Hint: There were many promises God made in the Old Testament about a coming Messiah and deliverer.)

21. Mears says, "Everyone who has heard the gospel must either accept the Lord as Savior or trample Him underfoot." How does Mark develop this theme? How does this challenge compare to the following attitudes?

    A lifelong churchgoer says, "Jesus was totally nonjudgmental and would never do anything to make people feel guilty."

A church member asks, "Do you believe in the Lordship of Christ?" His minister answers, "It's not for me to tell God how to be God."

22. It is vogue among some churchgoers today to say the essence of the gospel is "inclusiveness." Would Mark and Henrietta Mears agree?

In what ways is the gospel inclusive (i.e., for all peoples)?

In what ways is the gospel exclusive (i.e., not for everyone)?

If the gospel of Jesus is a message that requires people to admit they need a Savior rather than to persist in self-sufficiency, will the message of Jesus ever cease to divide people?

23. Henrietta Mears says regarding Mark 11:15–12:44 that "Jesus sought to persuade the Jews to receive Him as the Messiah." For generations Jewish leaders have tried to persuade the public that being Jewish and believing in Jesus are incompatible. Yet in Jesus' time, some Jews did believe in Him. The same is true today—there are some Jews who believe in Jesus, many of them now worshiping in messianic synagogues.

Do you know any messianic believers or synagogues? They often have wonderful insights into both the Old and New Testaments of the Bible, which are thoroughly Jewish books!

24. Henrietta Mears, reflecting on the attacks of Jesus' enemies that led to His death, says, "All the way through, the perfect servant of God was dogged by His enemies." What enemy or enemies exist today? What expectation should Christians have about opposition to the gospel?

THE SERVANT EXALTED (MARK 16)

The discussion concludes with Henrietta Mears's comments on the Great Commission.

25. Reflecting on the two versions of the Great Commission in Matthew and Mark, Mears says, "In Mark, we see in Jesus' words that His disciples are to take His place; and He will serve in and through them. He is yet the worker, though risen (see v. 20). The command rings with urgency of purpose—not a corner of the world is to be left unvisited, not a soul to be left out!"

How do obeying, following and supporting the Great Commission express love?

How does failure to obey, follow and support the Great Commission express lack of love?

26. Mark 10:45 says, "For even the Son of Man did not come to be served, but to serve, and to give his life as a

ransom for many." Even though Mark's Gospel emphasizes Jesus as the servant of God, look at how Jesus finishes in Mark 16:19: "After the Lord Jesus had spoken to them, he was taken up into heaven and he sat at the right hand of God."

The phrase "right hand" of God occurs throughout the New Testament (see Matt. 22:44; Mark 12:36; 14:62; Luke 20:42; 22:69; Acts 2:25,33-34; 5:31; 7:55-56; Rom. 8:34; Eph. 1:20; Col. 3:1; Heb. 1:3,13; 8:1; 10:12; 12:2; 1 Pet. 3:22). It is a staple of New Testament preaching and teaching. Look up these verses and verify for yourself the overriding importance of this fact of Christian faith.

Can you think of any implications for your own life from this stupendous fact?

CHAPTER 4

UNDERSTANDING Luke

Luke Portrays Jesus Christ, the Son of Man

The writer of this third Gospel was Dr. Luke, Paul's companion (see Phil. 1:24; Col. 4:14; 2 Tim. 4:11). He was a native of Syria and apparently not a Jew, for Colossians 4:14 places him with other Gentile Christians. If this is true, he was the only Gentile writer of the New Testament books.

It is easily seen that Luke was an educated man and a keen observer. Luke's Gospel was written for the Greeks. Besides the Jews and the Romans, the Greeks were another people who had been preparing for Christ's coming. They differed from the other two in that they possessed a wider culture and loved beauty, rhetoric and philosophy. Luke, an educated Greek himself, was well fitted for addressing this audience.

In Luke's introduction (see 1:1-4), the human element is

connected to God's revelation. Luke addressed his Gospel to a man named Theophilus. It is thought he was an influential Christian layman in Greece.

Whereas Matthew presents Christ as King to the Jews and Mark presents Him as servant of Jehovah to the Romans, Luke presents Jesus as the perfect man to the Greeks. This is the Gospel for the sinner. It highlights Christ's compassionate love in becoming man to save man.

In Luke, we see God manifest in the flesh. Luke deals with the humanity of our Lord. He reveals the Savior as a man with sympathies, feelings and growing powers—a Savior suited to all. In this Gospel, we see the God of glory coming down to our level, entering into our conditions and being subject to our circumstances.

Luke's Gospel depicts Christ's manhood. However, even though Christ mingles with men, He is in sharp contrast to them. He is the solitary God-man. There is as great a difference between Christ as the Son of man and we the sons of men, as there is Christ as the Son of God and we as the sons of God. The difference is not merely relative but absolute. Read the words of the angel to Mary: "So the holy one to be born" (Luke 1:35), which refers to our Lord's humanity. It is in stark contrast to our humanity, which in nature is unclean (see Isa. 64:6). The Son of God, when He became incarnate, was holy. Adam in his unfallen state was innocent, but Christ was holy.

In keeping with the theme of his Gospel, Dr. Luke has given us the fullest particulars concerning the miraculous birth of Jesus. We are grateful that our chief testimony concerning Christ's birth should come from a physician. Christ, the creator of this universe, entered this world like any other person. It is a mystery of mysteries, but enough facts are provided to let us see that the predictions came true.

Luke alone tells the story of the shepherds' visit (see 2:8-20). We learn from this Gospel that as a boy, Jesus developed naturally (see 2:40,52). As a child, He was subject to Joseph and Mary (see 2:51). There was no record of unhealthy or supernatural growth. Only Luke tells of Jesus' visit to the Temple when He was 12 years old.

Luke tell us that Jesus, as a man, toiled with His hands (see 6:1), wept over the city (see 19:41), "knelt down and prayed" (22:41) and knew anguish (see 22:44). All are strikingly human. Five out of six of the miracles Luke records are miracles of healing, including one—the healing Malchus's ear (see 22:51)—that only Luke describes.

Luke is the Gospel for the outcast on Earth. It is Luke who tells of the good Samaritan (see 10:30-37), the publican (see 18:9-14), the prodigal (see 15:11-24), Zacchaeus (see 19:2-9) and the thief on the cross (see 23:39-43). He is the writer who speaks most of womanhood (see 1—2). Luke records Jesus' compassion for the woman of Nain (see 7:11-17) and the depths of His mercy to the woman who was a sinner (see vv. 36-50). His regard for women and children is shown throughout the book (see 7:46; 8:2-3,41-50; 10:38-42; 11:27; 23:27-28).

Luke is a poetic book. It opens and closes with a song. The world has been singing ever since. Thank God for such a Gospel! It preserves the precious gems of Christian hymnology:

- Mary's Song (see 1:46-55)
- Zechariah's Song (see 1:68-79)
- Angels' Song (see 2:8-14)

Luke speaks more of the prayers of our Lord than any other Gospel writer. Prayer is the expression of human dependence on God. Why is there so much working and activity in the Church and yet so little result in positive conversions to God? The answer is simple: There is not enough private prayer. The cause of Christ does not need more working but more praying.

The hardest thing the Early Church had to learn was that the Gentiles would have full and free admission into the Kingdom and into the Church. Simeon taught this. Read Luke 2:32. Christ sent 72 disciples not to the lost sheep of the house of Israel alone but "to every town and place" (Luke 10:1). Jesus' entire ministry over the eastern side of Jordan was to the Gentiles.

Old Testament Promises and New Testament Fulfillment

I will extol the LORD at all times; his praise will always be on my lips. My soul will boast in the LORD; let the afflicted hear and rejoice (Ps. 34:1-2).

Yet I will rejoice in the LORD, I will be joyful in God my Savior (Hab. 3:18).

Though the LORD is on high, he looks upon the lowly, but the proud he knows from afar (Ps. 138:6).

And Mary said: "My soul glorifies the Lord and my spirit rejoices in God my Savior, for he has been mindful of the humble state of his servant. From now on all generations will call me blessed" (Luke 1:46-48).

THE PREPARATION OF THE SON OF MAN (LUKE 1:1—4:13)

The opening of this beautiful book is significant. A man is to be described; and the writer, Luke, will draw his good friend Theophilus into it. Luke tells Theophilus of his personal knowledge on the subject: "Therefore, since I myself have carefully investigated everything from the beginning" (1:3). He seems to bring something warmly human into his task of presenting the man Christ Jesus.

Luke's tone throughout the Gospel is of this world, like John's Gospel, which begins, "In the beginning was the Word, and the Word was with God, and the Word was God" (1:1). Luke, so different, begins like a simple story touching people with, "In the time of Herod king of Judea there was a priest named Zechariah" (1:5). As the story progresses, we are introduced to Christ's human sympathies and relationships that none of the other Gospels tell. We learn all about the circumstances that accompanied the birth and childhood of the holy babe and about the one who was sent as His forerunner. The birth of John the Baptist (see 1:57-80), the angels' song to the shepherds (see 2:8-20), the circumcision (see 2:21), the presentation in the Temple (see 2:22-38) and the story of 12-year-old Jesus (see 2:41-52) are all recorded here.

In Luke 2:1, Luke notes: "In those days Caesar Augustus issued a decree that a census should be taken of the entire Roman world." Then comes a fact that we would never find in Matthew: Joseph and Mary "went to his [Joseph's] own town to register" (v. 3). Luke is not revealing One who has claims to rule but One who is coming down in humility to be fully involved in human affairs.

Old Testament Promises

Your righteousness reaches to the skies, O God, you who have done great things. Who, O God, is like you? (Ps. 71:19).

He provided redemption for his people; he ordained his covenant forever—holy and awesome is his name (Ps. 111:9).

But showing love to a thousand generations of those who love me and keep my commandments (Exod. 20:6).

Sing to the LORD a new song, for he has done marvelous things; his right hand and his holy arm have worked salvation for him (Ps. 98:1).

You save the humble, but your eyes are on the haughty to bring them low (2 Sam. 22:28).

God brings to pass what the prophets had spoken. Micah said that Bethlehem was to be the birthplace of Jesus (see Mic. 5:2-5) because He was of the family of David. Yet Mary lived in Nazareth, a town one hundred miles away. God saw to it that Imperial Rome sent out a decree to compel Mary and Joseph to go to Bethlehem just as the child was to be born. Isn't it wonderful how God used the decree of a pagan monarch to bring to pass His prophecies! God still moves the hand of rulers to do His bidding.

Read on. We hear the angels' message to the watching shepherds, but we do not find the wise men asking for "the one who has been born king of the Jews" (Matt. 2:2). The angel tells the poor shepherds, "I bring you good news of great joy that will be for all the people. Today in the town of David a Savior [not a King] has been born to you" (Luke 2:10-11).

Why did the Father allow His blessed Son, now incarnate in the flesh, to be born in this lowly place? Luke is the only one of the four evangelists who touches on this point concerning His humanity.

Boyhood Days

"The child grew ... and the grace of God was upon him" (Luke 2:40). When Jesus was 12 years old, He traveled with His parents to Jerusalem to the feast, as every Jewish boy did at that age. "The boy Jesus stayed behind in Jerusalem, but they were unaware of it" (v. 43). How characteristic of a young boy! He was found sitting in the midst of the doctors, both hearing them and asking them questions (see v. 46). How intensely human this

New Testament Fulfillment

For the Mighty One has gone great things for me—holy is his name. His mercy extends to those who fear him, from generation to generation. He has performed mighty deeds with his arm; he has scattered those who are proud in their inmost thoughts. He has brought down rulers from their thrones but has lifted up the humble (Luke 1:49-52).

is! Yet we read, "Everyone who heard him was amazed at his understanding and his answers" (v. 47). Luke says that He was filled with wisdom. Although human, He was always more than a man—He was also God. We find Jesus' first words here:

Didn't you know I had to be in my Father's house? (v. 49).

Again we read, "Then he went down to Nazareth with them [Joseph and Mary] and was obedient to them. . . . And Jesus grew in wisdom and stature, and in favor with God and men" (vv. 51-52). All of these things are peculiar to Jesus as man, and

Old Testament Promises

For he satisfies the thirsty and fills the hungry with good things (Ps. 107:9).

He has remembered his love and his faithfulness to the house of Israel; all the ends of the earth have seen the salvation of our God (Ps. 98:3).

I swear by myself, declares the LORD, that because you have done this and have not withheld your son, your only son, I will surely bless you and make your descendants as numerous as the stars in the sky and as the sand on the seashore. Your descendants will take possession of the cities of their enemies, and through your offspring all nations on earth will be blessed, because you have obeyed me (Gen. 22:16-18).

Luke alone records them.

Eighteen years of silence followed. We read of John the Baptist preaching "a baptism of repentance for the forgiveness of sins" (3:3). Then Jesus came to be baptized. Only Luke tells us, "When all the people were being baptized, Jesus was baptized, too. And as he was praying, heaven was opened" (v. 21). He is linked with "all the people"—He came down to the level of humans. Matthew and Luke record the baptism of Jesus, but John omits it, for Christ is viewed as God's only Son. Here alone do we read of the age at which our Lord entered His public ministry (see v. 23).

Genealogy

The genealogy of Jesus in Luke is given at the time of His baptism and not at His birth (see 3:23-38). There are noticeable differences between the genealogy in Luke and that found in Matthew 1. In Matthew, we have the royal genealogy of the Son of David through Joseph. In Luke, we have Jesus' personal genealogy through Mary. In Matthew, His genealogy is traced forward from Abraham; in Luke, it is followed backward to Adam. Each is significant! Matthew shows Jesus' relation to the Jewish people; therefore, he goes back no further than Abraham—father of the Jewish nation. Luke is concerned with Jesus' connection to the human race; therefore, His genealogy is traced back to Adam—the father of the human family.

New Testament Fulfillment

He has filled the hungry with good things but has sent the rich away empty. He has helped his servant Israel, remembering to be merciful to Abraham and his descendants forever, even as he said to our fathers (Luke 1:53-55).

In Luke, our Lord's line is traced back to Adam and is no doubt His mother's line. Notice that Luke 3:23 does not say Jesus was the son of Joseph. What are the words? "So it was thought." In Matthew 1:16, where Joseph's genealogy is given, we find Joseph was the son of Jacob. Luke says Joseph was the son of Heli (see Luke 3:23). Joseph could not be the natural son of two men. Carefully note that the record does not state that Heli begat Joseph, so it is supposed that Joseph was the son by law (or son-in-law) of Heli. Heli is believed to have been Mary's father.

Additionally, the Davidic genealogy in Luke goes through Nathan, not Solomon. This too is important. The Messiah must be David's son and heir, "who as to his human nature was a descendant of David" (Rom. 1:3; see 2 Sam. 7:12-13; Acts 2:29-31). He must be a literal flesh and blood descendant. Therefore, Mary must be a member of David's house as well as Joseph's (see Luke 1:32).

Spirit

"Jesus, full of the Holy Spirit, returned from the Jordan and was led by the Spirit in the desert, where for forty days he was tempted by the devil" (Luke 4:1-2). Only here do we learn that the Savior was "full of the Holy Spirit" as He returned from His baptism. Next we find the account of His temptation. Luke also is the only one to tell us that "Jesus returned to Galilee in the power of the Spirit" (v. 14), which shows that Satan had utterly failed to break the fellowship of the Son of man with His Father in heaven.

As Jesus came forth from the fire of testing in the unabated power of the Spirit, so can we. Only as we are filled with His Spirit can we overcome temptation.

The purpose of the temptation was not to discover whether or not Jesus would yield to Satan but to demonstrate that He could not—to establish the fact that there was nothing in Him to which Satan could appeal (see John 14:30). The more a rose is crushed, the stronger its fragrance. Thus, the more the devil assaulted Christ, the more His perfections were revealed.

THE MINISTRY OF THE SON OF MAN
(LUKE 4:14—19)

Scan through Luke from 4:14, and find the events in Jesus' life recorded in succession.

Jesus' Ministry Around Galilee (4:14—9:50)

· Ministry in Nazareth, His hometown (see 4:16-30)

- Preaching in Capernaum (see 4:31-44)
- Call of Peter, James and John (see 5:1-11)
- Call of Matthew (see 5:27-32)
- The pharisees (see 6:1-11)
- The twelve apostles chosen (see 6:12-16)
- The disciples taught (see 6:17-49)
- Miracles (see 7:1-17)
- Discourses of the teacher (see 7:18-50)
- Parables (see 8:4-18)
- Real relatives (see 8:19-21)
- The sea calmed (see 8:22-25)
- The maniac healed (see 8:26-39)
- The woman made whole (see 8:40-48)
- Jairus's daughter restored (see 8:49-56)
- The Twelve commissioned (see 9:1-9)
- Five thousand fed (see 9:10-17)
- Peter's confession (see 9:18-21)
- The transfiguration (see 9:28-36)
- A lunatic healed (see 9:37-43)

Jesus' Ministry in Judea (9:51—19:27)

- The 72 commissioned (see 10:1-24)
- The question of the lawyer (see 10:25-37)
- Jesus' friends Martha and Mary (see 10:38-42)
- Disciples taught to pray (see 11:1-13)
- Seeking signs (see 11:14-36)
- The Pharisees denounced (see 11:37—12:12)
- The sin of greed (see 12:13-34)
- Repentance (see 13:1-9)

- The Kingdom of heaven (see 13:18-30)
- Jesus talks on hospitality (see 14:1-24)
- Jesus talks on self-denial (see 14:25-35)
- The Savior and the lost (see 15:1-32)
- The unjust steward (see 16:1-30)
- Jesus on His way to Jerusalem (see 16:31—19:27)

Jesus' Ministry in Jerusalem (19:28—24)

- Triumphal entry (see 19:28-38)
- Rulers question Jesus' authority (see 20:1—21:4)
- Future things (see 21:5-38)
- Jesus' last Passover (see 22:1-38)
- Jesus betrayed (see 22:39-53)
- Jesus tried before the high priest (see 22:54-62)
- Jesus tried before Pilate (see 23:1-25)
- Crucifixion (see 23:26-49)
- Burial (see 23:50-56)
- Resurrection (see 24:1-49)
- Ascension (see 24:50-53)

This list is not complete, of course, but it gives a bird's-eye view of the busy life of the Son of man on Earth. The keyword of His ministry is "compassion."

Following the temptation in Luke 4, Jesus "went to Nazareth, where he had been brought up, and on the Sabbath day he went into the synagogue, as was his custom. And he stood up to read" (v. 16). Being brought up is an important thing in life. We find that Jesus was accustomed to going to the synagogue on the Sabbath day. He had been reared in a godly home.

Jesus stated that God had anointed Him to preach deliverance to the captives, and to bring good tidings to the poor and brokenhearted (see vv. 18-19). He selected a text from Isaiah 61:1-2, which announced the purpose of His whole mission on Earth. He was commissioned and sent of God, and He was divinely qualified for His work. He is our kinsman-redeemer. He was made like us that He might deliver us. He became man that He might bring man close to God.

At this very early point in Jesus' ministry, we see those of His own hometown determining to kill Him (see Luke 4:28-30). "Isn't this Joseph's son? they asked" (v. 22). This is the first hint of His coming rejection. He proclaimed Himself to be the Messiah (see v. 21) and the people were angered that He should hint that their Messiah would also be sent to the Gentiles (see vv. 24-27). They believed God's grace was to be confined only to their

Old Testament Promise and New Testament Fulfillment

The Spirit of the Sovereign LORD is on me, beause the LORD has anointed me to preach good news to the poor. He has sent me to bind up the brokenhearted, to proclaim freedom for the captives and release from darkness for the prisoners, to proclaim the year of the LORD's favor and the day of vengeance of our God, to comfort all who mourn (Isa. 61:1-2).

"The Spirit of the Lord is on me, because he has anointed me to preach good news to the poor. He has sent me to proclaim freedom for the prisoners and recovery of sight for the blind, to release the oppressed, to proclaim the year of the Lord's favor." Then he rolled up the scroll, gave it back to the attendant and sat down. The eyes of everyone in the synagogue were fastened on him, and he began by saying to them, "Today this scripture is fulfilled in your hearing" (Luke 4:18-21).

own kind of people, and so they were ready to kill Him. He refused to work miracles for them because of their unbelief. They attempted to cast Him down the brow of the hill, but He escaped and went to Capernaum (see vv. 29-31).

A World Gospel

The Jewish people hated the Gentiles for having treated them harshly when they were captives in Babylon. They regarded the Gentiles with contempt. They considered them unclean and enemies of God. Luke pictures Jesus tearing down these barriers between Jews and Gentiles, making repentance and faith the only conditions of admission to the Kingdom:

> And repentance and forgiveness of sins will be preached in his name to all nations, beginning at Jerusalem (24:47).

The gospel of Jesus Christ is not just one of the religions of the world. It is the living truth of God, adapted to all nations and to all classes (see Rom. 1:16).

As the Son of man, Christ looks at the needs of the Gentiles as He looks at the needs of all people. In Luke 6, which in substance is the same as the Sermon on the Mount in Matthew, we find simple, broad moral teachings, suited to the needs and wants of all people. What Matthew put into three chapters, Luke condenses into a few verses (see vv. 20-49). Luke makes no reference to "the Law and the Prophets" (Matt. 7:12).

Jesus speaks choice words here to His disciples. The Beatitudes are a picture of the Christian. "Blessed are" begins each one. It is not what we are striving to be but who we are in Christ that brings us joy. The Beatitudes are a picture of Christ—the picture of the face of Jesus Himself.

Commissioned Disciples

When the Twelve are commissioned (see Luke 9:1-6), a broader field of ministry begins. In Matthew, we hear the Lord saying, "Do not go among the Gentiles or enter any town of the Samaritans. Go rather to the lost sheep of Israel" (10:5-6). Luke omits this and says:

> And he sent them out to preach the kingdom of God and to heal the sick. So they set out . . . preaching the gospel and healing people everywhere (9:2,6).

Wherever this man Christ Jesus went, a multitude followed Him and "tried to touch him, because power was coming from him and healing them all" (6:19). He gave of Himself. Our service must be of this kind.

We also find Jesus' power over disease and death (see 7:1-17). He had come "to seek and to save what was lost" (19:10). He is called "a friend of tax collectors and 'sinners'" (7:34).

Jesus Christ the Teacher

Jesus is not only recognized as a great healer but also acknowledged as a magnificent teacher.

The scholars—Jesus was a teacher. His disciples were taught and trained to carry on His message (see 6:12-16).

The school—Matriculation in this school is guarded. Prerequisites are demanded, but entrance is easy. There is no barrier of age, sex, race or color (see 14:25-33).

Entrance requirement—"And anyone who does not carry his cross and follow me cannot be my disciple" (14:27). "In the same way, any of you who does not give up everything he has cannot be my disciple" (14:33).

Examinations—Jesus knows the strengths and weaknesses of each student in His school. His examinations are not the same for everyone. He gives individual tests. For example, look at the tests Jesus administers to Peter. In Luke 5:4-8, He tests Peter on obedience. In Luke 9:18-20, Jesus springs an examination upon this impetuous fellow, and Peter gives a startling answer.

Rules—A right relationship with the teacher must be maintained at all times. Many people think that just because they have at one time entered into a relationship with the great teacher, this is all that is necessary. This is false. There must be a constant study of His Word, a laboratory time of prayer (see 11:1-4) and a gymnasium of spiritual exercise (see 5:27; 9:59).

A practice school—Jesus not only taught, but He also made His disciples try out the great facts He presented (see 10:1-12,25-28,30-37; 11:35; 12:8-9; 14:25-33; 18:18-30).

The course—The course includes a study of the Kingdom and the King (see 7:28; 8:1; 9:2,11,62; 12:31-32; 13:20-21,28-30; 17:20-21; 18:29-30; 19:12-26; 22:29).

THE SUFFERING OF THE SON OF MAN (LUKE 20—23:56)

Jesus is sitting with His disciples around the table, celebrating the feast of the Passover. At this time, He institutes what we call the Lord's Supper. Listen to His words:

> This is my body given for you. . . . This cup is the new covenant in my blood, which is poured out for you (Luke 22:19-20).

Old Testament Promise and New Testament Fulfillment

Even my close friend, whom I trusted, he who shared my bread, has lifted up his heel against me (Ps. 41:9).

Then Judas Iscariot, one of the Twelve, went to the chief priests to betray Jesus to them (Mark 14:10).

This is different from the account in Matthew and Mark, which read, "This is my blood of the covenant, which is poured out for many" (Matt. 26:28; Mark 14:24). His love is expressed in such a personal way in Luke. The evangelist adds these words of Jesus: "Do this in remembrance of me" (22:19).

See the sad record of events in connection with His death. We find the disciples arguing over which one of them should be counted greatest in the Kingdom (see 22:24-27). We follow Peter from that moment and read a lamentable story—one that ends in his denial of Jesus (see vv. 54-62).

Look into the garden of Gethsemane. Jesus is praying, and "his sweat as it were great drops of blood falling down to the ground" (v. 44, *KJV*). Luke tells us that the angels came to minister to Jesus, the Son of man (see v. 43). Matthew and Mark don't mention the ministering angels.

In the shadow of the garden, a band of soldiers approached, and leading them was Judas (see v. 47). He stepped up to kiss Jesus. Judas was a disciple, but the Scriptures had said that Jesus would be betrayed by a friend and sold for 30 pieces of silver (see Ps. 41:9; Zech. 11:12; Luke 22:47-54).

Worst of all, His other friends deserted Him. Peter denied Him, and all except John the beloved forsook Him and fled. Luke alone tells us that Jesus looked on Peter, the denier, and broke his heart with a look of love (see Luke 22:61-62).

We follow Jesus into Pilate's hall and then standing before Herod (see 23:1-12). We follow Him along the Via Dolorosa ("way of suffering") to the Cross (see vv. 27-38). Only Luke gives the name "Calvary" (v. 33, *KJV*), which is the Latin name for "Golgotha," meaning "skull." Luke omits much that Matthew and Mark record, but he alone gives the prayer (see v. 34).

There were three crosses on Calvary. On one of them was a thief dying for his crimes. Luke tells us this story, too (see vv. 39-43). The way this thief was saved is the way every sinner must be saved. He believed on the lamb of God who died on the Cross to pay the penalty of sin.

The scene closes with the Son of man crying with a loud voice, "Father, into your hands I commit my spirit" (v. 46). The centurion, in keeping with this Gospel, bears this witness, "Surely this was a righteous man" (v. 47).

THE VICTORY OF THE SON OF MAN (LUKE 24)

We turn with great relief from the sorrow and death of the Cross the darkness and gloom of the tomb to the brightness and glory of the resurrection morning.

Luke gives us a part of the scene Matthew and Mark leave untold. It is the story of the walk to Emmaus (see 24:13-35).

He shows that to the disciples, Jesus, as their resurrected Lord, was the same loving, understanding friend He had been before His death. After Jesus' walk and conversation with them, the disciples urged Him to come in and spend the night with them. He then revealed who He was when He lifted His hands, which had been pierced on the cross, and had broken the bread. At once they knew who He was, but He vanished. Upon returning to Jerusalem, the disciples found abundant proof of His resurrection. He proved to them that He was a real man with flesh and bones.

No fewer than 11 appearances of Jesus are recorded following His resurrection—not only to individuals, but also to companies and crowds. Jesus first appeared to the women, next to Mary Magdalene and then to others (see Mark 16; John 20:14). Then He appeared to Peter alone (see Luke 24:34), to two men walking to Emmaus (see Luke 24:13-16), to ten apostles in Jerusalem (see John 20:19) and subsequently to the eleven remaining disciples (see John 20:26,29). Moreover He later revealed Himself to seven men at the sea of Tiberias (see John 21:1) and again to the all the apostles on a mountain in Galilee (see Matt. 28:16), then to five hundred brethren at once (see 1 Cor. 15:6) and to James (see 1 Cor. 15:7) and finally to the little group on the Mount of Olives at His ascension (see Luke 24:51).

Three times, we are told, His disciples touched Him after He arose (see Matt. 28:9; Luke 24:39; John 20:27). He ate with them, too (see Luke 24:42; John 21:12-13).

As Jesus put out His hand to bless them, "he left them and

was taken up into heaven" (Luke 24:51).

He is no longer a local Christ, confined to Jerusalem, but He is a universal Christ. He said to His disciples who mourned for Him, thinking that after He left, He would be with them no more, "And surely I am with you always" (Matt. 28:20). How different the demeanor of His chosen followers on the day of ascension from their state of despair and shame at the crucifixion. They returned to Jerusalem with great joy.

STUDY GUIDE

If Matthew's audience was primarily Jewish people, and Mark's was Romans, who was Luke thinking of as he wrote?

Henrietta Mears mentions that Luke's intended audience was the Greeks and other people greatly influenced by Hellenistic culture and values. This can be a bit confusing, because a great deal of cultural accommodation, borrowing and intertwining was happening at the time. The prevailing culture in the Roman Empire was actually a Greco-Roman stew.

1. Studies of Greek mythology often focus on the ideal of human perfection and beauty. Did any Greek hero or god truly embody full perfection?

2. Greek art and drama examined the depths of human emotions and often played on the disparity between the nobility of man and his foolishness, pettiness and cruelty. Mears says that Luke "reveals the Savior as a

man with sympathies, feelings and growing powers—a Savior suited to all." Read Hebrews 2:5-18 for a poignant summary of how Jesus was made like us to bring us to God. What did the Son of God give up to become a man?

3. Jesus was unlike us in one very important aspect, and Henrietta Mears boils this down to one significant word—"perfect." Another way of saying this is found in Hebrews 4:15, which says Jesus "was without sin." This is in contrast to 1 John 1:8, which says, "If we claim to be without sin, we deceive ourselves and the truth is not in us." How can sinful people have a relationship with a perfect God?

4. Mears says, "Christ, the creator of this universe, entered this world like any other person." As amazing as it sounds, this is the clear testimony of Scripture. See John 1:1-3,14 and Colossians 1:15-17. When the Bible declares God made the heavens and the earth, the Son of God was intimately involved. The universe was made "by him and for him" (Col. 1:16). Who fashioned you and gave you life? Who sustains you every moment of your life? To whom do you owe your life?

5. The Bible teaches that God has always existed as God the Father, God the Son and God the Holy Spirit. The Incarnation is the teaching that God the Son took upon Himself human flesh and dwelt among us in order to make it possible to bring us back to God. Read

Psalm 113. Has God ever been an aloof, far-off God? How does Psalm 113 anticipate what Jesus did for us?

If Jesus grew up like us—toiled with His hands, laughed, wept and prayed—what does that mean for us as we pray?

6. The Bible teaches that Jesus grew up like us. Mears says, "There was no record of unhealthy or supernatural growth." What she means is that Jesus had a normal childhood. The authentic Gospels resist the temptation to embellish the record with giddy speculations. By contrast, some spurious gospels create fantastic and weird stories of Jesus' supposed miraculous powers as a child—in one He is supposed to have blown onto clay pigeons and made them alive! How would these wild stories diminish the authentic Gospels' representation of Jesus?

7. One profound result of the Incarnation is how it affirms human dignity of all people. Mears says, "Luke is the Gospel for the outcast on Earth." Then she talks about Luke's unique attitude toward women—an attitude that contrasted sharply with cultural attitudes toward women then and now. Have you ever felt like an outcast? Can you imagine how women or lepers felt when they were rejected or put down by society? How did Jesus raise up the outcasts?

8. The profound truth of the intrinsic worth of individuals

extends past the boundaries of the people of Israel. In Jewish tradition, the Gentiles (i.e., non-Jews) were seen as not only far from God (which was true) but also unloved by God (which is not what the Scriptures teach). According to Mears, what was one of the hardest lessons for the Early Church (which at first was primarily Jewish) to learn? Why?

Was Jesus' ministry only to Jews, or was it also directed toward Gentiles?

THE PREPARATION OF THE SON OF MAN (LUKE 1:1—4:13)

After Jesus' temptation by the devil in the wilderness, Mears gives us some pertinent spiritual application: "As Jesus came forth from the fire of testing in the unabated power of the Spirit, so can we. Only as we are filled with His Spirit can we overcome temptation."

9. Do you think the "unabated power of the Spirit" is only for super-Christians or for all Christians?

What role does temptation have in preparing, or enabling, us to be filled with the Holy Spirit?

Besides enabling us to overcome temptation, what does to be filled with "the unabated power of the Spirit" mean?

Is being filled with the unabated power of the Holy Spirit something Christians should shun or eagerly desire?

THE MINISTRY OF THE SON OF MAN (LUKE 4:14—19)

In this section, we are introduced to Jesus' divine mission.

10. We see that Jesus was brought up in a godly home. He was accustomed to going to synagogue on the day of worship. If it is important to be raised in a godly home, what if you missed out on that experience? Can God still use you?

11. Jesus quotes from Isaiah 61:1-2, which was a way of referencing all the promises God had made to His people. Read Isaiah 61:1-2. Notice the last phrase Jesus read. What does the fact that Jesus omitted the last phrase of Isaiah 61:2 tell you about Jesus' mission?

    What happens when the Spirit of the Lord is upon His servant?

12. Henrietta Mears says that Jesus "is our kinsman-redeemer." This phrase comes from Ruth 3:9; 4:14. A kinsman-redeemer was a close relative who had the right and the means to buy another out of slavery or debt. How has Jesus been a kinsman-redeemer for you?

13. Jesus anticipated that the people in His hometown would resist His message. He actually provoked them to reveal their hearts when He said that just as people did not believe the Old Testament prophets, so they also would have difficulty believing in Him. Jesus recounts an incident in which Elijah was sent to a Sidonian woman's house (a non-Jew). He also says that Naaman the Syrian (a non-Jew) was cleansed of his leprosy in the time of Elisha. How would these examples have gone against the expectations of the townspeople?

    Why would they have wanted to throw Jesus off a cliff? (Hint: See what Henrietta Mears says under "A World Gospel.")

14. Read Romans 1:16. Is there any indication in this verse that the gospel—God's Word—is just one of the religions of the world and that all of the world's religions are equal?

15. On the Beatitudes, Mears says: "It is not what we are striving to be but who we are in Christ that brings us joy. The Beatitudes are a picture of Christ—the picture of the face of Jesus Himself." In the New Testament, to be "in Christ" means to be spiritually united with Christ in His life, death, burial, resurrection and ascension to the right hand of the Father. How can your union with Christ bring you joy? How might your union with Christ bring you (godly) sorrow?

THE SUFFERING OF THE SON OF MAN
(LUKE 20:1—23:56)

Henrietta Mears takes us on an almost eyewitness tour of the last hours of Jesus' life. Periodically reflecting on Jesus' last days is something that all Christians need to do, soberly and reverently. The reason Jesus instituted the Last Supper is so that we would perpetually remember the cross until He comes again.

16. Read the Scripture passages in this section of Luke and try to imagine yourself in the moment, feeling everything: the weather, the nonverbal communication, the tones of voice, the tiredness, the layers of betrayal and abandonment, the prayers, the sweat, the blood, the wood and the iron.

    Henrietta Mears says the thief on the cross "was saved . . . the way every sinner must be saved." What way is that?

THE VICTORY OF THE SON OF MAN
(LUKE 24)

The first thing this section recounts is the story of the walk to Emmaus. The resurrected Christ walks with two disciples down the road to Emmaus, but they don't recognize Him. The key verse is Luke 24:26, *NASB*: "Was it not *necessary* for the

Christ to suffer these things and to enter into His glory?" (emphasis added).

17. A lot of people think the sacrifice of Christ on the cross for the sins of humanity was unnecessary and even barbaric. But according to Jesus, it was both *predicted* and *necessary*! Verse 27 says: "And beginning with Moses and all the Prophets, he explained to them what was said in all the Scriptures concerning himself." In Jewish tradition, "beginning with Moses" includes the first five books of the Bible attributed to Moses. "All the Prophets" indicates prophetic history from Joshua—where Moses' writing left off—to Malachi—the last book in the Bible. In other words, *Jesus was saying the whole Hebrew Bible pointed toward Himself!* The Messiah's coming wasn't an afterthought—Jesus' coming is the purpose of history! What do you think of this amazing claim?

Which Old Testament Scriptures do you think might point to Jesus, either in direct prophecies or in archetypes, symbols, tokens, signs, distinguishing characteristics, models, patterns, foreshadows or forms (see Gen. 22:1-18; Exod. 12; Deut. 18:18; Pss. 2; 16:9-11; 22; 110; Isa. 53)?

Why might people be offended by the idea that the atonement (i.e., Jesus' sacrifice for us) was necessary? What might be your response to these objections?

Why do you think Jesus thought it was necessary to die on the cross? Does it make you appreciate Him more, knowing that He knew what He would have to go through for us and then doing it anyway?

18. Notice what happens to the men: "Were not our hearts burning within us while he talked with us on the road and opened the Scriptures to us?" (v. 32). How do you react to this revelation about Christ in the Old Testament? Are you kind of blasé about it, or does it really fire you up?

19. The physical resurrection of Christ is a bedrock belief of Christian faith. In fact, apostle Paul says in 1 Corinthians 15:14: "If Christ has not been raised, our preaching is useless and so is your faith," and we might as well "eat and drink, for tomorrow we die" (15:32).

On what basis might people dismiss the Christian claim of the resurrection of Christ? Does it really matter if Christ was raised or not? Why or why not?

Read 1 Corinthians 15 in its entirety. Why do you think Paul made such a big deal about the resurrection of Christ? What is the point?

If Christ is alive now, sitting at the right hand of the Father, what are the implications for your life?

CHAPTER 5

UNDERSTANDING JOHN

John Portrays Jesus Christ, the Son of God

This Gospel opens with Christ in the bosom of the Father, and closes with John in the bosom of Christ.

ADONIRAM JUDSON GORDON (1846-1895), AMERICAN PASTOR,
MISSIONARY EXECUTIVE, AND EDUCATOR

The author, John, indicates the purpose of his Gospel in the opening 18 verses, the prologue. He also states it very plainly in John 20:31.

John wrote to prove that Jesus was the Christ—the promised Messiah for the Jews and the Son of God for the Gentiles—and to lead believers into a life of divine friendship with Him.

The keyword is "believe," which appears 98 times in John's Gospel.

The theme of John's Gospel is the deity of Jesus Christ. More here than anywhere else, His divine sonship is established. We are shown that the babe of Bethlehem was none other than "the One and Only, who came from the Father" (1:14). There is abundant proof. Even though "all things were made" by Him (v. 3) and "in him was life" (v. 4), He "became flesh and made his dwelling among us" (v. 14). "No one has ever seen" (v. 18) Him; therefore, Christ came to declare Him.

Old Testament Promise and New Testament Fulfillment

No man can see Me and live! (Exod. 33:20, NASB).

The Word became flesh and made his dwelling among us. We have seen his glory, the glory of the One and Only, who came from the Father, full of grace and truth (John 1:14).

Unlike the Synoptic Gospels—Matthew, Mark and Luke—John does not record:

- Christ's genealogy—neither His legal lineage through Joseph (see Matt. 1), nor His personal descent through Mary (see Luke 3:23-38)
- His birth—because He was "in the beginning" (John 1:1)
- His boyhood
- His temptation—Jesus rather is presented as Christ the Lord, not the One subject to all temptations like humans

- Christ's transfiguration
- Jesus' appointing of His disciples
- Jesus' parables
- Christ's ascension
- Our Lord's Great Commission

Yet only in John's Gospel is Jesus called:

- "The Word" (1:14)
- The creator (see 1:2-3)
- "The only begotten Son . . . of the Father" (1:18, *KJV*)
- "The Lamb of God" (1:29,36)
- The "I AM" (8:58; Exod. 3:14)

John was known as one of the "Sons of Thunder" (Mark 3:17) and "the disciple whom Jesus loved" (John 13:23; 21:7,20). His father was Zebedee, a successful fisherman; his mother was Salome, a devout follower of the Lord who may have been a sister of Mary, the mother of Jesus (see Mark 15:40; John 19:25). His brother was James. His position was probably somewhat higher than that of the ordinary fisherman.

John may have been about 25 years of age when Jesus called him. He had been a follower of John the Baptist. In the reign of the Roman emperor Domitian, John the disciple was banished to Patmos, an island off the coast of modern-day Turkey. Afterward, he returned to Ephesus and became the pastor of the wonderful church in Ephesus. He lived in Ephesus until he was an old man—the last of the 12 apostles. During this time, he wrote his Gospel concerning the deity of Christ.

John wrote nearly a generation after the other evangelists, somewhere between A.D. 80 and A.D. 100. At the end of the first century, all of the New Testament writings were complete except for John's writings. The life and work of Jesus were well known by that time. The gospel had been preached, Paul and Peter had suffered martyrdom, and all the apostles—save John—had died. Additionally, Jerusalem had been destroyed by the Roman legions under Titus.

The synoptic Gospels were written before A.D. 70, which marked the fateful year of the overthrow of Jerusalem. Already false teachers had arisen and denied that Jesus Christ was the unique Son of God come in the flesh. John, therefore, emphasized the facts, supplied the witnesses and recorded the words and works of Jesus that revealed His divine power and glory.

John's tone is more elevated and his view more exalted than that of the other Gospels. In each of the first three Gospels, Christ is viewed in human relationship with an earthly people, but in John we find Him in spiritual relationship with a heavenly people.

In Matthew and Luke, terms for Christ such as "Son of David" and "Son of man" link Him to humans on Earth. In John, "Son of God" connects Him with the Father in heaven.

In Luke, divine care was taken to guard our Lord's perfection in His humanity; however, in John, His deity is guarded. In days of widespread departure from the truth, the deity of Christ Jesus had to be emphasized.

In John, Jesus is shown dwelling with God before any creatures were formed (see 1:1-2). He is "the glory of the One and Only" (v. 14); "this is the Son of God" (v. 34). Jesus speaks of God as "my Father" 35 times. Twenty-five times He

Old Testament Promise and
New Testament Fulfillment

You will be like a well-watered
garden, like a spring whose
waters never fail (Isa. 58:11).

If anyone is thirsty, let him come
to me and drink. Whoever
believes in me, as the Scripture
has said, streams of living water
will flow from within him
(John 7:37-38).

says, "Verily, verily" (*KJV*)—speaking with authority. And besides Jesus' own affirmation, six different witnesses declare His deity.

JESUS' DEITY

In every chapter in John's Gospel we see Jesus' deity:

- Nathanael confesses, "You are the Son of God" (1:49).
- In the miracle of Cana, "He thus revealed his glory" (2:11).
- In His word to Nicodemus, He said He was "[God's] one and only Son" (3:16) or "his only begotten Son" (*KJV*).
- In His conversation with the woman of Samaria, He said, "I who speak to you am he [the Messiah]" (4:26).
- To the invalid man, He disclosed that "the voice of the Son of God" will call the dead to life (5:25).
- He admits, "I am the bread of life" (6:35).
- He proclaims, "If anyone is thirsty, let him come to me and drink" (7:37).
- To the unbelieving Jews, He disclosed, "Before Abraham was born, I am!" (8:58).
- The blind man was told, "You have now seen him [the Son of Man]; in fact, he is the one speaking with you"

(9:37), which is Jesus' unique claim to being the Son of God.

- Jesus stated, "I and the Father are one" (10:30).
- Martha declared, "You are the Christ, the Son of God" (11:27).
- To the Greeks, Jesus said, "But I, when I am lifted up from the earth, will draw all men to myself" (12:32).
- At the Last Supper, He said, "You call me 'Teacher' and 'Lord,' and rightly so, for that is what I am" (13:13).
- He makes the statement, "Trust in God; trust also in me" (14:1).
- Likening us to branches on a vine, He says, "Apart from me you can do nothing" (15:5).
- In promising the Holy Spirit, He says, "I will send him to you" (16:7).
- He prays to the Father, "Glorify your Son" (17:1).
- During His trial, He states, "You are right in saying I am a king" (18:37).
- During His atonement, He had the right to say, "It is finished" (19:30).
- In his confession, Thomas the doubter exclaimed, "My Lord and my God!" (20:28).
- In demanding obedience, Jesus stated, "You must follow me" (21:22).

Seven Witnesses

The Gospel of John was written so that people might believe that Jesus Christ was God. John brings seven witnesses to the stand to prove this fact. Let's turn to the Scriptures and hear each one make his or her own statement:

1. What do you say, John the Baptist? "This is the Son of God" (1:34).
2. What is your conclusion, Nathanael? "You are the Son of God; you are the King of Israel" (1:49).
3. What do you know, Peter? "You are the Holy One of God" (6:69).
4. What do you think, Martha? "You are the Christ, the Son of God" (11:27).
5. What is your verdict, Thomas? "My Lord and my God!" (20:28).
6. What is your statement, John? "Jesus is the Christ, the Son of God" (20:31).
7. What do You say of Yourself, Christ? "I am God's Son" (10:36).

Seven Miracles

Besides the seven witnesses in John, we find seven miracles, or signs, that prove He is God. "For no one could perform the miraculous signs you are doing if God were not with him," said Nicodemus (3:2).

Let's look over these signs as they occur in John's Gospel:

1. Turning water into wine (see 2:1-11)
2. Healing the nobleman's son (see 4:46-54)
3. Healing the man at Bethesda (see 5:1-15)
4. Feeding the five thousand (see 6:1-14)
5. Walking on water (see 6:15-21)

6. Healing the blind man (see 9)
7. Raising of Lazarus (see 11:17-45)

Seven "I Am's"

There is yet more proof of Jesus' deity presented by John. Jesus reveals His God nature in the "I am's" of John's Gospel:

1. "I am the bread of life" (6:35).
2. "I am the light of the world" (8:12).
3. "Before Abraham was born, I am" (8:58).
4. "I am the good shepherd" (10:11).
5. "I am the resurrection and the life" (11:25).
6. "I am the way and the truth and the life" (14:6).
7. "I am the true vine" (15:1).

Savior and Messiah

John alone records Jesus' triumphant shout, "It is finished" (19:30). The finished work of salvation is accomplished only by the Son of God. John also is the only evangelist to record the Samaritan townspeople's conclusion: "We know that this man really is the Savior of the world" (4:42).

John wrote his Gospel that people might believe that Jesus is the Christ. It was written especially for the Jews, in order to lead them into a personal belief in Jesus as the Messiah who came in fulfillment of all the Old Testament prophecies.

In John, Christ the Messiah is revealed. "Messiah" means "anointed One, who comes as divine King."

Consider again Nathanael who said, "Rabbi, you are the

Son of God; you are the King of Israel" (1:49).

To the woman at the well, Jesus declared Himself to be the long-expected Messiah (see 4:26).

To Pilate, Jesus testified that He was King (see 18:33-37).

Three Keys

Dr. Samuel Dickey Gordon (1859-1936), American author and international lecturer for the YMCA, and author of the *Quiet Talk* series, suggested: "There are three keys that unlock John's Gospel."

Backdoor key—This key unlocks the entire book. It states the purpose of the Gospel (see 20:31).

Side-door key—At the side, a bit toward the back, we find a second key. At the Last Supper with His disciples, Jesus reveals this truth to them: "I came from the Father and entered the world; now I am leaving the world and going back to the Father" (16:28). His constant thought was that He used to be with the Father. He came down to Earth on an errand and stayed for 33 years, but He would go back to His Father.

Front-door key—This key hangs right at the front—outside, low down, within every child's reach. "Yet to all who received him, to those who believed in his name, he gave the right to become children of God" (1:12). This is the primary key to the whole house. Its use permits the front door to be flung wide open. Anyone who believes may enter through this door.

THE GREAT PROLOGUE (JOHN 1:1-18)

When we start to read the Gospel of John, we must keep this

question in mind: "What do you think about the Christ?" (Matt. 22:42). Is He only the world's greatest teacher or is He actually God? Was He one of the prophets or is He the world's Savior whose coming was foretold by the prophets?

All that John discusses is crowded into the first 18 verses and summarized in John 20:31. Let's study this Gospel with John's purpose clearly in mind. As we read John 20:31 again, we can see how the plan is developed and how the purpose is shown.

The Son of God

John begins his wonderful record describing Jesus the Christ before His incarnation. God did not send His Son into the world in order that He *might* become His Son, for He *is* the eternal Son.

Comparing the first verses of John with the other three Gospels, we see how differently it opens—how exalted its theme is. John 1:1-18 opens like the book of Genesis. Omitting the birth of Jesus, the Son of man, John begins, "In the beginning" (1:1). Here Jesus is portrayed as the Son of God.

Our Lord had no beginning. He was in the beginning. He is eternal. Because Christ was before all things, He was not a part of creation—He *is* the creator (see Col. 1:16; Heb. 1:2).

"The Word was with God" (John 1:1). Christ is the second person of the Triune God (i.e., God has always existed as God the Father, God the Son and God the Holy Spirit). Jesus is called "the Word." He came to declare God and to tell about God. As words utter thoughts, so Christ utters God. As words reveal the heart and mind, so Christ expresses, manifests and shows God. Jesus said to Philip, "If you really knew me, you would know my Father as well" (14:7).

Then comes the wonderful announcement that "through him all things were made; without him nothing was made that has been made. In him was life, and that life was the light of men" (1:3-4). Yes, "the Word became flesh and made his dwelling among us" (v. 14). The full claims of Christ are given here: truly God, light of life, declarer of God the Father and baptizer with the Holy Spirit.

The Son of Man

John does not open with the manger scene in Bethlehem but before all worlds were formed: "In the beginning" (1:1). Jesus was the Son of God before He became flesh and dwelt among us.

When Christ became the Son of man, He did not cease to be God. He was God-man. He lived in a tabernacle of flesh on Earth for 33 years. "Incarnation" comes from two Latin words, *in* and *caro*, meaning "flesh." Therefore, Christ was God in the flesh.

People sinned and lost the image of God, so Christ "the image of the invisible God" (Col. 1:15) came to dwell in people. We cannot see God; therefore, "the only begotten Son, which is in the bosom of the Father" (John 1:18, *KJV*) came to declare Him to us.

Even the witness of John the Baptist is different in John's Gospel. In Matthew, John tells of the coming Kingdom. In Luke, he preaches repentance. In John, he is a witness to Jesus, the light, that all men might believe (see 1:7). He points to "the Lamb of God" (v. 36).

Jesus is God Himself in human form, coming to Earth. Jesus is the witness of the Father to humans. Jesus knows the

Father. He has lived with Him from the beginning. He came to Earth to tell us what He knows. He wants humans to know the Father as He knows Him.

He speaks to us by His words, deeds, character and love—but most of all by His dying on the cross and His rising the third day. This is a declaration, a witness and a spoken word.

How was Christ the Word received? Read John 1:11: "He came to that which was his own, but his own did not receive him." Christ presented Himself as Messiah and King to His people, but He was rejected. All through the Gospel we see Jesus dividing the crowds. As He comes out and speaks the truth, the crowds listen. Some believe and some reject. John's Gospel presents the results of some believers' faith.

In essence, John's prologue deals with Christ before His incarnation. Jesus is none other than God manifest in the flesh. We see Christ drawing people to Himself (see 12:32). Remember, John is writing to prove that Jesus is the Son of God.

The Way of Salvation

How can we receive salvation?

Believe and receive (see 1:12)

What is the result of salvation?

We become a child of God (see 1:12).

What can't we count upon for salvation?

Natural descent—heredity (see 1:13)

Human decision—culture and education (see 1:13)

The will of man—prestige or influence (see 1:13)

What can we count upon for salvation?

God—the power of the Holy Spirit (God comes down and redeems us if we believe and receive only Him as Savior and Lord [see 1:13].)

PUBLIC MINISTRY (JOHN 1:19–12)

The great drama of John's Gospel begins when John the Baptist steps onto the scene: "Among those born of women there has not risen anyone greater than John the Baptist," declares Jesus (Matt. 11:11; see Luke 7:28). John is the fore-runner of the Messiah. In this Gospel, John the Baptist is not described. He merely bears his witness that Jesus is the Messiah (see 1:19-34).

A delegation of priests and Levites are sent to ask John who he claims to be. He tells them he is not the Messiah; he is not even Elijah or another prophet of whom Moses spoke. John is merely "the voice of one calling in the desert, 'Make straight the way for the Lord'" (v. 23).

The next day, when he sees Jesus, John points to Him and says, "Look, the Lamb of God" (v. 29).

Then John the Baptist indicates that he knows Jesus is the Messiah because he "saw the Spirit come down from heaven as a dove and remain on him" (v. 32). John adds, "I have seen and I testify that this is the Son of God" (v. 34).

Jesus Cleanses the Temple

Jesus' disciples were convinced of His deity by His first miracle—turning water into wine. He spoke and it was so. This was the first sign to prove He was the Messiah (see 2:11).

Old Testament Promise and New Testament Fulfillment

God himself will provide the lamb for the burnt offering (Gen. 22:8).

Behold, the Lamb of God who takes away the sin of the world! (John 1:29, NASB).

There was only one place where Jesus could start His ministry—in Jerusalem, the capital city. Prior to the Passover, the Lord entered the Temple; and taking a whip of cords as a badge of His authority, He cleansed the sanctuary, which He declared to be His Father's house. By this act, He claimed to be the Son of God (see vv. 12-25).

When the rulers asked Jesus for a sign to prove His authority—after Jesus cleansed the Temple and drove out the money changers—He said, "Destroy this temple, and I will raise it again in three days" (v. 19). The rulers were shocked because it had taken 46 years to build this edifice. "But the temple he had spoken of was his body" (v. 21). The supreme proof of Christ's deity is the resurrection.

Jesus Teaches Nicodemus

Jesus taught Nicodemus the wonderful facts about eternal life and His love (see 3:16) and the new birth (see v. 6). Nicodemus was a moral, upright man, yet Christ said to him, "You must be

**Old Testament Promise and
New Testament Fulfillment**

*Love the LORD your God with
all your heart and with all your
soul and with all your strength
(Deut. 6:5).*

*The Father judges no one, but
has entrusted all judgment to the
Son, that all may honor the Son
just as they honor the Father. He
who does not honor the Son does
not honor the Father, who sent
him (John 5:22-23).*

born again" (v. 7). If Jesus had said this to the Samaritan woman, Nicodemus would have agreed with Him. She was not a Jew. On the other hand, Nicodemus was a Jew by birth and he had a right to expect favor. Yet Jesus told him that he "must be born again" in order to enter the kingdom of heaven.

Have you been born again?

Like the Jewish people of his day, Nicodemus knew God's law but nothing of God's love. He was a moral man. He recognized Jesus as a teacher, but he did not know Him as a Savior. Nicodemus's failure to recognize Jesus as God is shared by many people today. They put Jesus at the head of the list of great teachers, but they do not worship Him as the one true God.

Jesus Speaks with a Samaritan Woman

Jesus revealed to one woman the truth—He is the source of all life. This story gives us Christ's estimate of a single soul. He brought an immoral woman face-to-face with Himself and showed her what kind of life she had been leading. Her conditional view of marriage was not unlike that of many people today. Christ did not condemn her or pass judgment upon her, but He revealed to her that He was the only One who could meet her needs. He alone satisfies. The wells of the world bring no satisfaction. Did the woman believe Christ? What did she do? Her actions spoke louder than any words. She returned home and by her simple testimony brought a whole town to Christ (see 4:4-42).

Old Testament Promise and New Testament Fulfillment

When the dew settled on the camp at night, the manna also came down (Num. 11:9).

I am the bread of life. He who comes to me will never go hungry, and he who believes in me will never be thirsty (John 6:35).

Jesus Heals Nobility

In healing the son of a royal official, Jesus gives another sign of His deity. During His interview with the centurion, Jesus brought him to an open confession of Christ as Lord, and his whole household joined with him (see 4:46-54).

Jesus Feeds the Five Thousand

The miracle of feeding five thousand people was not a parable Jesus told but one that He performed. Jesus Himself was the Bread of Life. He wanted to tell all who put their trust in Him that He would give satisfaction and joy (see 6:35).

The people wanted to make Christ their King because He could feed them. Isn't that like people today! They long for someone who can give them food and clothing. However, Christ would not be King on their terms. He dismissed the excited multitude and went to a mountain. The people were

disappointed that He would not be a political leader, so they "turned back and no longer followed him" (v. 66).

The people were divided over Jesus (see 7:40-44). We see unbelief developing into hostility, but in His true followers faith was growing. We must decide today if Jesus is "the way and the truth and the life" (14:6). Either He is God or He is an impostor. There is no middle ground.

Jesus Heals the Blind Man

Jesus' healing of the blind man allowed Him to reveal Himself—"the light of the world" (9:5)—to the blind man and to His disciples. When the Pharisees cast the blind man out because of his confession of Christ (see vv. 13-34), Jesus gave a great discourse on the Good Shepherd (see 10:1-18). People had varied and extreme reactions to Christ's words (see vv. 19-21). Notice that many accused Christ of blasphemy after He said, " 'I and the Father are one.' Again the Jews picked up stones to stone him" (vv. 30-31). However, what happened to many people despite all of the criticism and opposition (see v. 42)?

Jesus Raises Lazarus from the Dead

The raising of Lazarus is the final sign in John's Gospel (see 11:38-44). The other Gospels record the raising of Jairus's daughter and of the son of the widow of Nain. What makes this situation different is that Lazarus has been dead four days. In reality, it is not harder for God to raise someone who has been dead longer; nevertheless, this peculiar circumstance has a profound effect on the leaders (see 11:47-48). In addition, the great claim Jesus made for Himself to Martha is recorded here:

Old Testament Promise and New Testament Fulfillment

I know that my Redeemer lives, and that in the end he will stand upon the earth. And after my skin has been destroyed, yet in my flesh I will see God (Job 19:25-26).

I am the resurrection and the life. He who believes in me will live, even though he dies (John 11:25).

> I am the resurrection and the life. He who believes in me will live, even though he dies; and whoever lives and believes in me will never die. Do you believe this? (vv. 25-26).

The scene closes with Jesus' triumphant entry into Jerusalem (see 12:12-18). His public ministry has come to an end. It is recorded that many of the top Jewish leaders believed in Him without making an open confession (see v. 42).

Jesus Makes Startling Claims

Jesus claims to be equal with God. He calls God "my Father" (5:17). The Jews knew what He meant, because they knew Jesus claimed God as His Father in a unique sense.

Jesus claims to be the light of the world. "I am the light of the

Old Testament Promise and New Testament Fulfillment

I AM WHO I AM (Exod. 3:14).

"I tell you the truth," Jesus answered, "before Abraham was born, I am!" (John 8:58)

world. Whoever follows me will never walk in darkness, but will have the light of life" (8:12).

Jesus claims to be eternal with God. "'I tell you the truth,' Jesus answered, 'before Abraham was born, I am!'" (8:58). This claim of having been with God always is unambiguous. He is either the Son of God or an impostor. Indeed, He uses the "I AM" of God's personal name (Exod. 3:14), equating Himself with the Father. No wonder the Jews "picked up stones to stone him" (John 8:59).

PRIVATE MINISTRY (JOHN 13—17)

Here we leave the multitude behind and follow Jesus as He lived the last week of His life on Earth before His crucifixion. We call it Passion Week:

Sunday—the triumphant entry into Jerusalem
Monday—the cleansing of the Temple
Tuesday—the conflicts in the Temple; the discourse on the Mount of Olives
Thursday—preparation for the Passover; the Last Supper with His disciples

The Last Evening Together

Last words are always important. Before Jesus leaves, He gives His disciples His last instructions, commonly known as the holy of holies of the Scriptures. We need to prayerfully read John 13—17 all in one sitting.

Jesus gathered His own around Him in the Upper Room and told them many secrets before He departed from them. He wanted to comfort His disciples, for He knew how hard it would be for them when He was gone. They would be sheep without a shepherd.

It is wonderful that Jesus selected and loved men like these. They seem to be a collection of nobodies with the exception of Peter and John, yet they were "his own" (13:1), and He loved them. One of Jesus' specialties is to make somebodies out of nobodies. This is what He did with His first group of followers, and this is what He has continued to do throughout the centuries.

What a picture we have in John 13:1-11. Jesus, the Son of God, girded with a towel and holding a basin of water in His blessed hands, is washing His disciples' feet! He wants us to serve in the same spirit. He teaches us that greatness is always measured by service. There is no loving others without living for others (see vv. 16-17). Christ said, "The greatest among you will be your servant" (Matt. 23:11).

Jesus foretells His betrayal by Judas, and Judas goes out into the night. Judas's heart is dark (see John 13:18-30). Fellowship brings light. Sin brings darkness. Although his opportunities for knowing Jesus were unsurpassed, he rejects the Lord, choosing sin and darkness over fellowship and light. This is what unbelief can do. Belief means life; unbelief means death.

After announcing His going, the Lord gives His disciples a new commandment to love one another:

> A new command I give you: Love one another. As I have loved you, so you must love one another. By this all men will know that you are my disciples, if you love one another (vv. 34-35).

Discipleship is tested not by the creed we recite, not by the hymns we sing and not by the rituals we observe; it is tested by our love for one another. The measure in which Christians love one another is the measure in which the world believes in them and their Christ. It is the final test of discipleship. (Jesus also mentions this new commandment in John 15:12.)

Christ's Answer for a Life Beyond Death

"I am going there to prepare a place for you.... I will come back and take you to be with me" (14:2-3). This is Jesus' cure for heart trouble—faith in God. We see there is no break between John 13—14. Jesus moves right on to His discourse. Many hearts have been put to rest and many eyes have been dried by Jesus' words in John 14.

At this point, Jesus already had mentioned His Father, but now He talks about the other person of the Godhead— the Holy Spirit. When Christ leaves, He will send the Comforter who will abide with believers. This is a wonderful promise for the child of God! Jesus repeats the promise in John 15:26 and again in John 16:7-16. Today too few people have the Holy Spirit present in their lives, yet it is by His power that we live. Never call the Holy Spirit "it." He is a person. He is One of three persons in the Trinity.

"Peace I leave with you; my peace I give you" (14:27). This is Christ's legacy to us. The only peace we can enjoy in this world is His peace.

Jesus reveals the real secret of the Christian life to His disciples in John 15:4: "Remain in me, and I will remain in you." He is the source of life. We must abide in Christ as the branch abides in the vine. The branch cannot sever itself—it must abide if it is to bear fruit. This is the picture of life in Christ. If we live and walk in Christ, we will bear fruit. If we are not abiding in Christ, we will not bear fruit.

After Jesus ended His talk with the 11 disciples, Jesus spoke to the Father (see 17). The disciples listened to His loving and solemn words. They must have been thrilled when Jesus told the Father how much He loved them and cared for them. He mentioned to the Father everything that He had taught them. He also asked the Father to protect them (see v. 11), sanctify them (see v. 17), make them one (see v. 21) and let all His children share in His glory some day (see v. 24).

If we grasp the beauty and depth of these wonderful words, let us kneel and let the Son of God lead us in prayer as we read aloud John 17.

Let's briefly look at John's teaching about the Holy Spirit:

1. *The incoming Spirit*: This is the commencement of the Christian life, the new birth by the Spirit. We are born by the Spirit into the family of God (see 3:5).
2. *The indwelling Spirit*: He fills us with His presence and brings us joy (see 4:14).

3. *The overflowing Spirit*: "Streams of living water will flow from within him" (7:38)—not just little streams of blessing, but rivers—if the Holy Spirit dwells within us.

4. *The witnessing Spirit*: He speaks through us. This particular task of the Christian—to testify of Christ—occurs through the Holy Spirit (see 14—16).

SUFFERING AND DEATH (JOHN 18—19)

Judas's Betrayal

Immediately following Jesus' prayer, He went into the garden of Gethsemane, "knowing all that was going to happen to him" (18:4). The change of scene from the Upper Room to the garden was like going from light to darkness. Only two hours had passed since Judas left the Last Supper to betray his best friend, something he was not forced to do. Judas personally chose to betray Christ, and this treacherous act fulfilled prophecy. No one ever had to sin to carry out God's plan.

The hour had come! The mission of our Lord on Earth was ending. The greatest work of Christ remained to be done. He was to die in order to glorify the Father and save the sinful world. He came "to give his life as a ransom for many" (Matt. 20:28; Mark 10:45). Christ came into the world by a manger and left it by the cross.

Jesus was now ready to give the real sign of His authority in answer to the question in John 2:18-19: " 'What miraculous sign can you show us to prove your authority to do all this?'

Jesus answered them, 'Destroy this temple, and I will raise it again in three days.'"

We see Jesus, always poised and always gentle. He knew His hour had come. He was not surprised when He heard the soldiers approach. He stepped forward to meet them. The men retreated and fell before the majesty of His look (see 18:4-9).

Then, bound as a captive, Jesus was brought to the hall of the high priest. However, Jesus was the One in command of the situation throughout this terrible drama. He went forth as a voluntary sacrifice (see v. 4). He deliberately tasted death for each one of us.

Peter's Denial

Almost as sad as Judas's betrayal was Peter's denial (see 18:15-18,25-27). Peter deserted Jesus in His hour of need, denying three times that he had any connection with his best friend.

Peter's denial is a lesson for all of us in the danger of overconfidence. Peter did not know that the supreme trial of his life would come from a servant girl's question (see v. 17), but trials in our life often occur when we least expect them. We lock and bolt the main door, but the thief breaks into the bedroom window we forgot to latch.

Disciples' Desertion

All of the disciples except John deserted Jesus in the hour of His greatest need. (Peter denied Jesus, but he stayed close by.) However, we shouldn't start blaming them. Suppose we look up and see where we are. Are we following Jesus closely? Can Christ count on us?

Last Moments

Jesus finally arrived at the supreme, crowning act of His life on Earth. It was not a crisis but a climax. He came to Earth "to give his life as a ransom for many" (Matt. 20:28; Mark 10:45).

Finally, the make-believe trials are over. It is morning at last, and yet it seems like night. It is the world's blackest hour. The courtyard is deserted. The fire at which Peter warmed himself is only gray ashes. The soldiers' jeers, Herod's sneers and Pilate's indecision are over.

The brief interval between Peter's denial and Jesus' climb to Golgotha was crowded with incidents. The night trial before Caiaphas and the Sanhedrin, a court of 70 religious rulers, probably preceded the last denial of Peter. Then came the awful treatment that lasted until the morning session of the Sanhedrin.

Often the cruel scourging of the Romans was so severe that prisoners died under the torturing blows. The crown of thorns thrust upon Jesus' holy brow was only one of many acts of cruel torture. When He comes again, He will bring many crowns (see Rev. 19:12).

Then Pilate led Him forth and said, "Here is the man!" (John 19:5). What a sight! To see the creator of this universe—the light and life of the world, the holy One—treated so. Satan energized the religious rulers, and they cried, "Crucify! Crucify! . . . he claimed to be the Son of God" (vv. 6-7).

Jesus was crucified at "the place of the skull" (v. 17)—Golgotha. Salvation is costly—"Christ died for our sins" (1 Cor. 15:3)—it cost Him His life.

At the Cross, we have hate's record at its worst and love's record at its best. People so hated that they put Christ to death. God so loved that He gave people life.

Our religion is one of four letters instead of two. Other religions say, "Do." Our religion says, "Done." Our Savior already has done the work on the cross—He bore our sins. When He gave up His life, He said, "It is finished" (John 19:30). This is the shout of a conqueror. He has finished human's redemption. Nothing is left for people to do. Has the work been done in our hearts?

Old Testament Promise and New Testament Fulfillment

"This is the covenant I will make with the house of Israel after that time," declares the LORD. "I will put my law in their minds and write it on their hearts. I will be their God, and they will be my people" (Jer. 31:33).

And with that he breathed on them and said, "Receive the Holy Spirit" (John 20:22).

VICTORY OVER DEATH (JOHN 20—21)

We have a Savior who is victorious over death. On the third day, the tomb was empty! The grave clothes were all in order, but the body was missing. Jesus had risen from the dead but not as others had done. When Lazarus came forth, he was bound in his grave clothes. He came out in his natural body; he was not a spirit. However, when Jesus came forth, His natural body had been changed to a spiritual body (see Luke 24:39). The changed body left behind its linen wrappings, as a butterfly leaves its chrysalis shell (see John 20:6-8).

Jesus' appearances—11 in all after His resurrection—helped His disciples to believe that He was God. Read the confession

of the sixth witness, Thomas the doubter (see v. 28). Jesus wanted each one of His disciples to be free from doubt, because they
had to carry out His Great Commission and take the gospel
into all the world (see v. 21).

Jesus even gave Peter an opportunity to confess Him as
Lord three times (see 21:15-17). When Peter did, Jesus restored
him to full privileges of service. Christ only wants those who
love Him to serve Him. If we love Him, we must serve Him. No
one who loves Christ can help but serve.

One of Jesus' last statements in John's Gospel is "Follow
me!" (v. 19). This is His word to each one of us. May we all follow Him in loving obedience until He returns (see v. 23).

STUDY GUIDE

Before beginning this study of the Gospel of John, it is important to understand some Old Testament concepts about God,
how John's Gospel relates to those concepts and Henrietta
Mears's commentary on them.

The book of Exodus depicts God leading the Israelites out
of Egypt with miracles and wonders. Moses regularly pauses
and asks the Lord for guidance at what he calls "the tent of
meeting" (Exod. 33:7). On one occasion the Lord promises,
"My Presence will go with you" (33:14). Then Moses boldly
asks, "Show me your glory" (v. 18).

The Lord replies, "'I will cause all my goodness to pass in
front of you, and I will proclaim my name, the LORD, in your
presence. I will have mercy on whom I will have mercy, and I

will have compassion on whom I have compassion. But,' he said, 'you cannot see my face, for no one may see me and live'" (vv. 19-20).

1. Why would coming face-to-face with God have been such an awesome, holy, terrifying and dangerous experience?

2. The following are other passages in the Old Testament that describe people seeing God. Look these verses up and then write down what these episodes have in common.

   • Genesis 32:24-30—Jacob wrestles with God.

   • Exodus 3:6—God spoke to Moses at the burning bush.

   • Exodus 24:9-11—The 70 elders of Israel eat and drink before God.

   • Judges 6:22-23—Gideon sees the angel of the Lord face-to-face.

   • Judges 13:22—Manoah, Samson's father, sees the angel of the Lord.

3. The above passages are the background to John 1:18. Referring to this verse, Henrietta Mears says, "We cannot see God." Read John 1:18. What is unique about

Jesus compared to God the Father, whom Old Testament believers saw in some powerful, life-threatening and life-transforming way but did not die?

4. The Old Testament says the beginning of wisdom is the fear of the Lord (see Prov. 1:7). How does Exodus 33:20 relate to the fear, reverence and respect for God we see in the Bible? What do these Old Testament passages suggest about undue familiarity with the awesome, holy God?

5. Read John 1:17. Moses was and remains the most prominent human figure in all of Judaism. Why? How does John compare Jesus with Moses? What is Jesus able to do that Moses could not?

Mears mentions that John's Gospel was written *after* the fateful events of A.D. 70. Titus, the Roman general, utterly destroyed Jerusalem and its Temple after a horrible siege. Titus also banished the Jewish people from Jerusalem and its environs. The significance of this military defeat had huge consequences for the history of the Jewish people.

The reason for the great loss is that before A.D. 70, Judaism had been a Temple religion. Every morning and evening animal sacrifices were made for sins small and large. The Temple was the center of community, religious, civil and political life. Festivals were held at the Temple. We must remember that Herod's Temple—called by Jewish historians the Second Temple (the first was Solomon's Temple)—was a bona fide wonder of the ancient world. The people had great pride in the Temple—the center of their lives.

6. After A.D. 70, the Jews were decimated. Without Temple, sacrifices, the priesthood (ancestral records having been destroyed) and their main city, and forbidden to enter or come near their once glorious city, they were left hopeless and mourned the thousands dead. Try to imagine what a devastating blow this was. What impact might this event have had on the Early Church members, many of whom were Jewish believers in Jesus? What impact might it have had on John himself?

7. Read Matthew 24:2 and Luke 19:44. Jesus actually predicted in graphic terms this very defeat. He foresaw the end of the sacrificial system and the ruin of the beautiful Temple. The New Testament book of Hebrews (written before A.D. 70) follows Jesus' lead, anticipating the disappearance of the Old Covenant and the old sacrificial system. Read Hebrews 8:13 and Hebrews 10. Why does the author of Hebrews say this would happen?

8. John's Gospel does not mention the events of A.D. 70 directly, but as you read, there are hints of the implications of the fall of Jerusalem and the destruction of the Temple. For example, John is the first Gospel writer to mention that John the Baptist (a different John than the author of John's Gospel) had very early called Jesus "the Lamb of God, who takes away the sin of the world!" (1:29). Given the Temple sacrifices and the

yearly Passover festival in which many lambs were sac-
rificed, what might the Jews have thought about this
declaration?

JESUS' DEITY

Mears mentions, "In days of widespread departure from the
truth, the deity of Christ Jesus had to be emphasized." If this
was true in the past, it is certainly more true today. Listen to
the words of the Episcopal bishop of New Jersey, John S.
Spong, a man who at one time actually took vows to defend the
Christian faith! After he denied that we can believe in a theistic
God (i.e., God is maker of heaven and Earth), Spong says:

> It is nonsensical to seek to understand Jesus as the
> incarnation of the theistic deity. So the Christology of
> the ages is bankrupt.
>
> The virgin birth, understood as literal biology,
> makes Christ's divinity, as traditionally understood,
> impossible.
>
> The view of the cross as the sacrifice for the sins of
> the world is a barbarian idea based on primitive con-
> cepts of God and must be dismissed.[1]

9. John Spong may be a very charming, charismatic, intelligent fellow. But if denials of core Christian truths like
   this are coming *from church leaders within the churches,*
   what can you do to be on your guard against such false
   teachers?

10. Can you think of any other examples of false teaching that go against the core Christian truths that you have heard from other church leaders? How can church members hold these leaders accountable for promoting errors that go directly against the clear teaching of Scripture?

11. What is your response to those who object to the deity of Christ by saying that Jesus never claimed to be God?

12. Under "Three Keys," Mears tells us that Dr. Gordon suggested a wonderful truth regarding John 1:12. The "front-door key" that opens the door to a relationship with God "hangs right at the front—outside, low down, within every child's reach."

    Isn't it great to know that you don't have to have a great intellect to be right with God? Even children can respond to the love of God. Do you know any children that you can share the gospel with today?

    Faith is the great key that flings the door of salvation wide open. If anyone can enter through faith, does this make Christian faith basically optimistic or pessimistic?

THE GREAT PROLOGUE (JOHN 1:1-18)

The great prologue is one of the most important passages in the whole Bible. Read John 1:1-18 in its entirety.

13. What is significant to you about the great prologue? What jumps out at you?

14. Henrietta Mears mentions that "John 1:1-18 opens like the book of Genesis."

    How does John 1 open like Genesis 1? What are some word and thought parallels?

    What happens when God speaks the word in Genesis 1? How might God's Word in Genesis be related to Jesus, the Word of God, in John 1?

    In Genesis 1, God's Word perfectly expresses God's personal will. How might Jesus, the Word of God, also fulfill that role?

15. There are various ways the term "Word of God" is used in the Bible. The Word of God (or Word of the Lord) may be revealed to a prophet of God; the Old Testament as a whole may be called the Word of God; the New Testament preaching of the gospel or revelation of truth can be called the Word of God; and here in John's Gospel Jesus Himself is called the Word of God. What is similar and what is different about these various uses of the term? If Jesus is the Word behind all these other true words of God, what ought to be your response to hearing the Word of God?

16. Some religious teachers at the time of John were happy to talk eloquently about God's Word but were offended

by the idea that the Word would sully itself by taking on flesh. They believed that spirit was good and flesh was evil, promoting the idea that the spirit of man was imprisoned in the prison-house of the body. Read John 1:14 and 1 John 4:2 (a short letter also written by John). How would John have responded to these false teachers' feelings?

17. All of the titles we get for Jesus from this great prologue are remarkable. Mears mentions: "truly God, light of life, declarer of God the Father and baptizer with the Holy Spirit." Is Jesus your true God? Is He the light of your life? Has He declared God's goodness to you? Has He baptized you with the Holy Spirit? If you're not sure, ask Him to be these things to you right now!

Understanding the Son of Man

Mears explains that "when Christ became the Son of man [at the Incarnation], He did not cease to be God. He was God-man." This concept must be accepted by faith; it will not ever be adequately understood. The disciples at first experienced Jesus as a man; but through His character, miracles, teaching and finally, his death and resurrection, they gradually came to understand who He really was.

18. You now have seen what the Bible clearly teaches about Jesus. Do you personally think He was just another prophet, like Unitarianism and Islam teach, or do you believe He is the unique Son of God? Do you think it

is legitimate to put Christ alongside religious teachers like Muhammad and Buddha, or is Christ totally unique in all of history?

19. According to Genesis 1:26-27, God created man and woman in His image. This certainly does *not* mean, as the Mormons teach, that God has a physical body and that the god of *this* world is the glorified Adam. The Mormon church also teaches that we have a physical "heavenly father" (Adam), as well as a physical "heavenly mother" (Eve). Mormon teaching says that if you are good Mormons you and your spouse can be the heavenly father and mother of other worlds. From what you have learned, can Mormonism legitimately be called monotheistic?

20. Genesis 1:26 actually means that humans have rational, spiritual, relational, creative and moral capacities that reflect God Himself. Therefore, all people—even the weak, the poor and the outcasts—have intrinsic worth and dignity. When we sin, we not only act against God, but we also act against what it means to be truly human (i.e., created in God's image). We violate our human dignity. Henrietta Mears says, "People sinned and lost the image of God, so Christ 'the image of the invisible God' (Col. 1:15) came to dwell in people." In your life today, how can the living Christ more fully restore the image of God (lost through sin) in you?

Placing Our Faith in Jesus

Mears quotes the paradoxical statement of John 1:11: "He came to that which was his own [i.e., the Jewish people], but his own did not receive him." This is actually an overstatement, since we know many of "his own" did put their trust in Jesus:

- The 12 apostles, the women who followed Him and many in the crowds believed in Jesus.
- Nicodemus (see 3:1-8; 7:50-52) and Joseph of Arimathea (see 19:38-42)—two leading Jewish figures in Jerusalem—believed in Jesus.
- "Many even among the leaders believed in him," according to John 12:42.
- For the first two decades of the Jesus Movement, almost all of His followers were Jewish!

However, belief in Jesus and confessing Him as Lord are sometimes complex.

21. Isaiah 6:9-10 is quoted in all four Gospels (see Matt. 13:14-15; Mark 4:12; Luke 8:10; John 12:40-41). Isaiah wrote about 750 years before Christ. What complaint did he have against the future generation that would largely reject the Messiah?

22. Read John 12:42-43. It appears that there was a lot of pressure to keep silent about belief in Jesus, especially among the Pharisees. Why do you think this was so? What would have been the cost of making a public declaration of belief in Jesus?

23. Read John 16:31. Jesus says to His disciples, "You believe at last!" What were the disciples doing before this time? Disbelieving? Or do you think they were gradually growing in their belief?

24. Mears makes the point that the message of Jesus will always divide the crowds. Some will believe; some will reject. What does this mean for you regarding preaching and living out the gospel in the world? Are you to hold back and not proclaim the gospel because some will not like it?

    How should you respond if some people reject Jesus? How are people ever going to hear the gospel if you do not take personal responsibility for spreading the good news of Jesus?

Clarifying Salvation

Mears explains in further detail what people need to count on for salvation.

25. A lot of people think they are Christians simply because they are born into a Christian family or culture, or because their ethnic group is Christian, as opposed to Buddhist, Islamic or polytheistic. What does John 1:13 say about this kind of thinking?

PRIVATE MINISTRY (JOHN 13—17)

Henrietta Mears calls John 13—17 "the holy of holies of the Scriptures." The phrase "holy of holies" comes from the holiest part of the Temple—the place closed to the public and to which the high priest only went once a year in a terribly formal, solemn ceremony. It was where the Ark of the Covenant rested—the box built to hold artifacts from Israel's earliest history, over which two statues of angels hovered and where the manifest presence of God, the Shechinah Glory, would periodically shine.

26. Take some time to read through John 13—17. Why do you think Mears chose the phrase "holy of holies" to describe this section of John's Gospel?

27. There are many wonderful things Jesus teaches in John 13—17. What is the greatest promise of these chapters to you? (Hint: Read John 14:12,16-18,26; 15:26; 16:7.)

    Why was it to the disciples' advantage that Jesus left (i.e., died on the cross)? Was it just to forgive them their sins or to send them to heaven after they died? Or was it for more? When the Holy Spirit is with you, who also is with you?

Note

1. John S. Spong, "A Call for a New Reformation," *CCLEC Publications.* http://www.episcopalian.org/cclec/paper-newreformation.htm (accessed September 2003).

CHAPTER 6

UNDERSTANDING acts

Acts Portrays Jesus Christ, the Living Lord

Luke, in his Gospel, shows what Christ began to do on Earth; Acts shows what He continued to do by the Holy Spirit.

The ascension of our Lord is the closing scene in Luke (see 24:49-51). It is the opening fact in Acts (see 1:10-11).

GOSPELS VERSUS ACTS

The Gospels present the Son of Man, who came to die for our sins. Acts shows the coming of the Son of God in the power of the Holy Spirit.

The Gospels establish what Christ began to do. Acts

reveals what He continued to do by the Holy Spirit, through His disciples.

The Gospels tell of the crucified and risen Savior. Acts portrays Him as the ascended and exalted Lord and leader.

In the Gospels, we hear Christ's teachings. In Acts, we see the effect of His teachings on the acts of the apostles.

Acts is not a record of the acts of the apostles; no extensive accounts are given of any of the apostles except Peter and Paul. Instead, Acts records the acts of the Holy Spirit through the apostles. His name is mentioned about 70 times. Look for some work of the Holy Spirit in every chapter of this book.

The word "witness" is used more than 30 times. "You will be my witnesses" (1:8) is the heart of the book of Acts. Salvation comes to this world through Christ alone (see 4:12); hence, people must know Him. Christ's plan includes us.

Are we witnessing for Christ? If not, why not? It is true that Christ alone can save the world, but Christ cannot save this world alone. If we have never witnessed for Christ, we need to look into our hearts, "for out of the overflow of the heart the mouth speaks" (Matt. 12:34).

Christ told His disciples that He would send the Spirit, and "he will testify about me. And you also must testify, for you have been with me from the beginning" (John 15:26-27). This promise from Christ was fulfilled on the Day of Pentecost when He poured the Holy Spirit upon the disciples (see Acts 2:1-4). From that moment forward, as the disciples bore witness to the Savior, the Holy Spirit bore witness to the hearts of their hearers; and multitudes came to the Lord.

It is a wonderful thing to know that when the Spirit

prompts us to speak to someone about Christ, He has been working in that person's heart and making it ready to receive our witness. There is a perfect example of this in Acts 8:26-40, which describes Philip's being sent to speak to the Ethiopian. Read this thrilling story!

What was the result of the first sermon on the Day of Pentecost (see 2:37-41)?

Isn't it amazing that in one generation the apostles had moved out in every direction and had preached in every nation of the then-known world (see Col. 1:23)? In each widening circle of influence, we find a marked outpouring of the Holy Spirit.

Old Testament Promise and New Testament Fulfillment

And everyone who calls on the name of the LORD will be saved (Joel 2:32).

When the people heard this, they were cut to the heart and said to Peter and the other apostles, "Brothers, what shall we do?" (Acts 2:37).

The infant Church was slow to realize the extent of its commission. Early believers confined their preaching to Jerusalem until persecution drove them out (see Acts 1—8:1). The blood of Stephen, the first Christian martyr, proved to be the seed of the growing Church.

The book opens with the preaching of the gospel in Jerusalem, the metropolis of the Jewish nation. It closes with the preaching of the gospel in Rome, the true metropolis of world power.

There are two natural divisions in Acts. In Acts 1—12, Peter says to the Jews, "Repent." Why? Because they needed a definite

change of mind about the Messiah. In Acts 13—28, Paul says, "Believe." Why? Because the Gentiles needed, not to change their minds concerning the Messiah, but to believe in Him.

The book also tells of the extension of the gospel to the Gentiles. Throughout the Old Testament, we find God primarily dealing with the Jewish people. In the New Testament, we find Him working among all nations.

No doubt Acts is the best guidebook to missions that has ever been written. In it we find the motive for missions. The believers' aim was to bring people to a saving knowledge of Jesus Christ. He was their one theme, and the Word of God was their one weapon.

We find the Early Church pursuing a definite program in carrying out its plans. Early Christians chose a great radiating center of population as a base from which the influence of their work might spread to the surrounding areas.

The disciples were simple, straightforward and successful. They depended entirely upon the power of God, through His Spirit. They moved with an unquenchable zeal and an unflinching courage.

POWER FOR WITNESSING (ACTS 1—2)

The disciples spent a wonderful 40 days with the Lord after His resurrection but before His ascension. How eager they were to hear His last words of instruction! He "spoke about the kingdom of God" (1:3). It was then that Jesus "gave them this command: 'Do not leave Jerusalem, but wait for the gift my Father promised, which you have heard me speak about'" (v. 4).

The first 11 verses of Acts 1 introduce the rest of the book:

- The Great Commission (see vv. 6-8)
- The Ascension (see vv. 2,9)
- The promise of Christ's return (see vv. 10-11)

The disciples still were not satisfied regarding Christ's plan for establishing His kingdom on Earth. They expected a kingdom that would give them political independence and establish them in a place of leadership in the world (see 1:6). What was Jesus' answer (see v. 7)?

One day as Jesus "led them out to the vicinity of Bethany, he lifted up his hands and blessed them" (Luke 24:50). He told them their power was to be spiritual and not political. Read His words:

> But you will receive power when the Holy Spirit comes on you; and you will be my witnesses in Jerusalem, and in all Judea and Samaria, and to the ends of the earth (Acts 1:8).

At Christ's ascension, our Lord went out of sight but stayed with the people in a far more real way. After He had spoken His last words to His disciples, He was taken up "and a cloud hid him from their sight" (v. 9). So great an event told in such few words! The Father took His Son back to glory.

Christ's Return

"This same Jesus . . . will come back in the same way you have seen him go into heaven" (1: 11). How will Jesus' coming back occur? Will it be merely at death? Is it as He comes to dwell in our hearts? No. The promise is that He "will come back in the same way." If this is true, we should examine how He left. Then we will know how He will come back. Jesus' return will be

- personal (see 1 Thess. 4:16),
- visible (see Rev. 1:7), and
- bodily (see Matt. 24:30).

Picture the disciples as they returned from the Mount of Olives to Jerusalem. They went into the Upper Room (see Acts 1:12-13). It might have been the same room where Jesus ate the Last Supper with them (see Luke 22:12). "They all joined together constantly in prayer" (Acts 1:14). Even though they had trained three years with the Lord, they needed the presence of the Holy Spirit, whom Jesus said He would send to empower them. They had proved to be a weak group in themselves.

Jesus had told them to stay in Jerusalem until they received "power from on high" (Luke 24:49). It would have been natural for them to flee from the place of Christ's crucifixion and to return to Galilee. But Christ said, "Tarry ye in the city of Jerusalem" (Luke 24:49, *KJV*), because it was the center of widest influence. We cannot always choose our place of service.

Next in importance to the coming of the Lord Jesus Christ to Earth was the coming of the Holy Spirit. The Church was born on the Day of Pentecost. We need to become familiar with this account given in Acts 2:1-13. Pentecost was one of the most popular Jewish feasts, so Jerusalem was crowded with pilgrims from near and far. It was 50 days after the Crucifixion. From this point forward, however, Pentecost was not to be a Jewish feast but the dawn of a new day—the birthday of the Church of Christ.

The scene opens with the disciples assembled together, their hearts fixed on Christ, as they wait for His promise to be fulfilled. The Holy Spirit Himself descended that day. Luke says there was "a sound like the blowing of a violent wind . . . [and] what seemed to be tongues of fire that separated and came to rest on each of them" (2:2-3). Fire is a symbol of divine presence; it illuminated and purified, and expressed the power to witness. The wind conveyed heavenly power. (See the results of this in verses 6 and 12.)

The Holy Spirit at Pentecost
The Spirit fell on (see 2:1-3), filled them (see v. 4) and worked through the early Christians who had gathered in the Upper Room (see vv. 41-47).

They were filled with the Holy Spirit and thus endowed for special service. They not only were enabled to preach in power, but they also could speak in the different languages represented that day at Jerusalem (see vv. 2-4).

The wonderful thing about Pentecost was not the "blowing of a violent wind" or the "tongues of fire," but the disciples' being filled with the Holy Spirit, that they might be witnesses to all people. If we do not have the desire to tell others of Christ, it is evident that we do not know the fullness of the Holy Spirit.

Do not think that on the Day of Pentecost the Holy Spirit came to the world for the first time. Throughout the Old Testament, we see accounts of how He had guided people and given them strength. Now the Spirit was to use a new instrument, the Church, which was born on that day.

The people gathered in the Upper Room were "amazed and perplexed" (v. 12). People by nature are unbelieving. Is it not a great exhibition of God's grace when people truly come to believe in God and accept His Word?

Some mocked: "They have had too much wine" (v. 13). People always try to explain away the miracles of God on natural grounds. Yet rationalism never provides a reasonable explanation of anything divine. Also, it was only nine in the morning, and no Jew could touch wine so early. Read Peter's defense against this false charge in verses 14 to 21.

Peter's Sermon

The theme of Acts 2:14-21, the first sermon in Acts, was that Jesus is the Messiah, as shown by His resurrection.

Peter is the prominent figure in the first 12 chapters of Acts. The real power of the Holy Spirit was shown when Peter, the humble fisherman, rose to speak and 3,000 souls were saved! How can we account for cowardly Peter's boldness as he stood that day to preach before a multitude on the streets of Jerusalem? What was the secret of Peter's ministry?

It took courage to charge men with murder; yet Peter did just this (see v. 36). Did he get away with it? Was he stoned? Verses 37 to 47 answer the questions.

"And the Lord added to their number daily those who were being saved" (v. 47). The First Church of Jerusalem, organized with a membership of 3,000 on the Day of Pentecost, was quite a church! Glorious days followed—in teaching and fellowship, signs and wonders, and, above all, salvation. This is the real objective of the Church. Are we seeing it today in our churches?

Daily life in the First Church was just as marvelous as the gift of tongues. It is not surprising that early believers found "the favor of all the people. And the Lord added to their number daily" (v. 47).

Old Testament Promise and New Testament Fulfillment

I will pour out my Spirit on all people. Your sons and daughters will prophesy, your old men will dream dreams, your young men will see visions. Even on my servants, both men and women, I will pour out my Spirit in those days (Joel 2:28-29).

These men are not drunk, as you suppose. It's only nine in the morning! No, this is what was spoken by the prophet Joel (Acts 2:15-16).

These first Christians were "regular" Christians:

- Regular in church going—"All the believers were together" (v. 44).
- Regular in church giving—"Selling their possessions and goods, they gave to anyone as he had need" (v. 45).
- Regular in church mission—"Every day they continued to meet together in the temple courts. They broke

Old Testament Promise and New Testament Fulfillment

Why do the nations conspire and the peoples plot in vain? The kings of the earth take their stand and the rulers gather together against the LORD and against his Anointed One (Ps. 2:1-2).

Now, Lord, consider their threats and enable your servants to speak your word with great boldness. Stretch out your hand to heal and perform miraculous signs and wonders through the name of your holy servant Jesus (Acts 4:29-30).

bread in their homes and ate together with glad and sincere hearts, praising God and enjoying the favor of all of the people. And the Lord added to their number daily those who were being saved" (vv. 46-47).

WITNESSING IN JERUSALEM (ACTS 3—8:3)

Acts chapter 3 opens at the beautiful gate of the Temple. Peter healed an incurable cripple, lame from birth, who had been carried daily to the Temple gate to beg for his living (see vv. 2-8). The miracle attracted the notice of the Jewish leaders and resulted in the first real opposition to the Church.

When a great crowd gathered around the lame man, who had been miraculously healed, Peter took advantage of the circumstances to preach his second recorded sermon. He did not spare his countrymen. Again he told them that Christ, whom they had crucified, was the long-promised Messiah (see vv. 12-26). The words of Peter and John were so powerful that a total of five thousand men turned to Christ (see 4:4)!

The leaders were "greatly disturbed" because the apostles taught the people that this Jesus rose from the dead and would appear again (see v. 2). They commanded the apostles not to preach and seized them, yet opposition made the Church thrive. Opposition should never be a matter of amazement—not even a surprise to any Christian. The work of the Spirit is always a signal for Satan to work. Whenever the Spirit comes to bless, the adversary comes to curse. Martyrdom is an aid to the Church, and whenever the truth is faithfully preached, fruit will come forth (see vv. 3-4).

As soon as the rulers released Peter and John, they sought their friends, reported their experiences and united in prayer and praise. While the Church must expect opposition, we can find courage and help in God in all circumstances:

> The place where they were meeting was shaken. And they were all filled with the Holy Spirit and spoke the word of God boldly (v. 31).

We find that this kind of bold speaking of the Word brought unity to the Church. They were "one in heart and mind" (v. 32); they went out "to testify to the resurrection of the Lord Jesus" (v. 33).

Let us speak out! Dying people need to hear; the day demands it!

Denying Self

In the Early Church people were not compelled to part with their personal possessions. Giving was a purely voluntary act on the part of the individual, not obligatory or expected; and it was not confined to Jerusalem, not temporary and not limited to believers.

The Church became so unselfish that many members sold all they had and gave the money to the apostles to distribute as people had need (see 2:45). But this act of love and generosity was open to abuse and deception. While Barnabas's generosity was an illustration of the spirit of love (see 4:36-37), Ananias and Sapphira were an illustration of deception in that they deceived themselves and the apostles. Yet the Holy Spirit revealed the truth: Ananias and Sapphira wanted glory without paying the price. They wanted honor without honesty. They were punished with instant death, because they claimed to have given all to God but actually did not (see 5:1-5).

As Christians, we claim to give all to Christ—to die to self. Complete surrender is the condition He sets down for discipleship—to "give up everything" and follow Him (Luke 14:33). Do we hold back from Christ? Are we hypocrites in our own testimony?

Modeling After Christ

The power in the apostles' story lies in the fact that they made their lives fit in with the life of their risen Christ. "You've got to show me" is the attitude of people in the world today. These early Christians did show the world. Do we show the world by our lives and conduct that we are Christians?

When signs and wonders were orchestrated among the people, the crowds came to see. When the Holy Spirit was in their midst, the people saw the power of God. The same is true today. When churches present Christ in His winsomeness and the Holy Spirit in His power, the people come. Christ draws all.

Miracles commonly result in converts. Just look in Acts. When the miracle of tongues occurred, the people thronged to the place (see 2:5). When Peter healed the crippled man at the Temple gate, "all the people were astonished and came running to them in the place called Solomon's Colonnade" (3:11). When the miracle of judgment came upon Ananias and Sapphira, "more and more men and women believed in the Lord and were added to their number" (5:14). We find these occurrences throughout the book of Acts.

Serving Christ

Thousands of articles have been written about how to put people to work in churches. There will be plenty of service in the church when we give first priority to the Holy Spirit. The Spirit-filled church will be a serving church.

Again we see in Acts 5:17-18 that the wonderful work of the apostles aroused the opposition of the Sanhedrin: "Then the high priest and all his associates . . . arrested the apostles and put them in the public jail." A few unlearned fishermen had risen up to teach, and multitudes listened and followed after them; hence, the religious leaders were disturbed. Even though the apostles were beaten with rods and prohibited from preaching, we find them rejoicing in the fact that they had been counted worthy enough to suffer shame for His name:

> Day after day, in the temple courts and from house to house, they never stopped teaching and proclaiming the good news that Jesus is the Christ (v. 42).

We find their boldest words in this statement: "We must obey God rather than men!" (v. 29). Is this the conviction of our lives? Let us have the spirit of these apostles! Let us not be discouraged when our opponents multiply.

Influencing the Church

Beginning in Acts 6, a meeting of the Church was called, and seven members were elected as deacons (see vv. 1-7). Two different offices in the Church formed: (1) "to wait on tables" (v. 2)—to benevolently care for the needy; and (2) to be devoted to preaching and prayer (see v. 4).

The first two deacons named were Stephen and Philip (see v. 5). These two men were mighty in their influence over the Church, perhaps more so than anyone else besides Peter and Paul.

The opposition was centered around Stephen (see Acts 6—7). He was just a layman, but he was one of the first deacons. He is described as a man "full of God's grace and power" (6:8). We have a record of only the last day of his life. What an account it is! It is not the length of time we live that counts, but how we live life. Someone once said that "a Christian is always on duty." This means that every minute of our lives is important and under God's direction.

Like thousands of other laypeople since his time, Stephen "did great wonders" because he was "full of faith and power" (v. 8, *KJV*). His life and death had an incalculable effect upon the history of the world, because he influenced the life of Saul of Tarsus. Who knows how our lives may affect a friend?

The leaders in the synagogue "could not stand up against his wisdom or the Spirit by whom he spoke" (v. 10). Their

anger flared into murderous hatred. Stephen was the first martyr of the Christian Church. To Stephen's death we can trace,
without doubt, one of the most outstanding impressions made
by a follower of Christ on an unbeliever—in this case, Saul (see
22:20).

WITNESSING IN JUDEA AND SAMARIA (ACTS 8:4—12)

The disciples were witnessing in Jerusalem, but Jesus had told
them they must go into Judea and Samaria.

If we were quite sure that we would lose our lives by
remaining in our hometown but would be safe in some nearby
village, would we go to that village? This is the very problem
that faced the Early Church in Jerusalem. Religious leaders
thought they were doing God's will when they tried to wipe out
the new sect by killing and imprisoning Jewish believers in
Jesus—followers of "the Way" (9:2). Paul said: "I too was convinced that I ought to do all that was possible to oppose the
name of Jesus of Nazareth" (26:9).

At that point, Paul really began his work of spreading the
gospel, but he did not know it. Paul was stamping out what he
considered to be a heretical and dangerous group (see 8:3).
Instead, he was spreading it:

Those who had been scattered preached the word
wherever they went (v. 4).

This is the reason the gospel spread at first. What commission
did the disciples have? "Go into all the world and preach the

good news to all creation" (Mark 16:15). How many disciples did Jesus train for His work? Just the Twelve, and one of them forsook Him.

Here were the Twelve, sitting down at Jerusalem, and "all the world" needed to hear the gospel. Saul's persecution, like the confusion of tongues at the tower of Babel, scattered the Christians throughout the world. Cowardice did not prompt them to flee, for every place we find them preaching the gospel.

We need to just laugh when we see anyone opposing the gospel. Persecution almost always spreads the gospel like wind spreads fire. This has occurred down through the centuries since our Lord lived on Earth.

Philip, the Evangelist

Philip (not the apostle), one of the seven deacons (see Acts 6:5), was an evangelist. He settled in Samaria as a result of the persecution. Jesus had said, "You will be my witnesses . . . in Samaria" (1:8). Philip preached about Christ. Multitudes followed him in his evangelistic campaign, but God called him to leave his successful work and "go south to the road—the desert road—that goes down from Jerusalem to Gaza" (8:26). Philip obeyed and left, and on the way he met an Ethiopian. This was not by chance. When we are in the will of God, things do not just happen by coincidence. No friend crosses your path by accident. No joy or sorrow comes into our lives except by God's permission.

This story raises a question: Which brings larger results—preaching to people in great numbers or telling people individually about the Lord? Some people think that winning just one person at a time to Christ would be a slow process, but listen to this!

Today there are approximately 280 million people living in the United States. Suppose there is only one living Christian among these 280 million people. That believer wins one soul of the 280 million today. Then tomorrow each of the two believers wins one soul for Christ. The following day, each of the four does the same; and the next day the eight win one apiece. Here is a startling fact: If each of these Christians and the newly won Christians were to win one soul a day to Christ, how long would it take to win 280 million? Less than one month (about 30 days) from the day the first one began! Wouldn't it be a good idea for us and our friends and church to form a G. O. Club—a Get One Club? This is Christ's method of soul winning.

Philip's Ethiopian convert no doubt preached the gospel in Africa. There is no evidence that Africa previously had any knowledge of the Son of God. The gospel was on its way to "the uttermost part of the earth" (1:8, *KJV*).

Saul

At Stephen's death, we have the first mention of Saul. Stephen's martyrdom seemed to inflame this persecutor of the Church. Saul was struggling with an awakened conscience. It was as if Saul knew he was in the wrong, but he would not give up. This is why Jesus told Saul in his vision: "It is hard for you to kick against the goads" (26:14).

Saul wreaked havoc on the Church! The more moral and intelligent a person is, the more harm that person can do when controlled by Satan.

The story of Saul's conversion is one of the most thrilling accounts in history. He was a man "breathing out murderous threats against the Lord's disciples" (9:1), yet soon afterward we find him preaching "in the synagogues that Jesus is the Son of God" (v. 20).

At every step of his three great missionary journeys, Paul made known Christ's will with unmistakable clarity. There is no doubt that Paul holds the most important place of any man in the New Testament. He was converted and made an apostle by Christ Himself. Christ gave firsthand revelations of truth to Paul, and to him Christ committed the doctrine of the Church. To what people was Paul especially sent? He was the apostle to the Gentiles, as Peter had been to the Jews.

Peter

What had Peter done since Pentecost? It is not only what a person believes but also what he or she is doing about it that counts. Christ told Peter that he was to be a witness. Peter helped start the Early Church, worked miracles and baptized thousands. His work was among the Jewish people.

After Pentecost, we find Peter in the house of Simon the tanner (see 10:5-6). God showed Peter that the gospel was for the Gentiles as well as the Jews (see vv. 9-16). The high wall of religious difference between Jew and Gentile had to be broken down. Peter was the man God used to start leveling it. Christ was building the Church, and He wanted both Jews and Gentiles to be the living stones of which it was to be formed (see Eph. 2:19-22).

At Pentecost, Peter used the "keys of the kingdom" (Matt. 16:19) entrusted to him to open the door of the gospel to the Jews. While Paul was in Tarsus, Peter was in the house of Cornelius, inserting the key into the lock of the door and opening it to the Gentiles (see Acts 10). As we read this account, let's think about racial prejudice. Was what God told Peter to do easy (see vv. 14-16)? Is the Church being inclusive today?

WITNESSING IN EARTH'S UTTERMOST PARTS (ACTS 13–28)

The death of Stephen was only the beginning of great persecution of Jesus' believers, most of whom were Jewish. How did they ever get to Antioch (see Acts 11:19-21)? Someone has called the Church in the early days "A

> **Old Testament Promise and New Testament Fulfillment**
>
> *I will also make you a light for the Gentiles, that you may bring my salvation to the ends of the earth (Isa. 49:6).*
>
> *When the Gentiles heard this, they were glad and honored the word of the Lord; and all who were appointed for eternal life believed (Acts 13:48).*

Tale of Two Cities," referring to Jerusalem and Antioch.

Up through Acts 12, we see the beginning of the Church in Jerusalem, with Peter as its leader. From Acts 13 to 28, we see Paul and the Church at Antioch—the new base of operations. Paul's wonderful missionary journeys started from Antioch, not from Jerusalem, because Antioch became the new center of the Church for carrying out Jesus' Great Commission.

In Antioch, the Jewish believers in Jesus who had been compelled to leave Jerusalem because of persecution were naturally thrown in with all the Gentiles, and they could not help but talk about that which interested them most. The power of the Lord

was so manifest that a great crowd joined the Church (see 11:21).

It was here in this church that a new name was given to Christ's disciples. They "were called Christians first at Antioch" (v. 26).

At this point, it is interesting to note that the Church had lost track of Paul. They did not know what had become of him, but Barnabas looked him up (see v. 25). If not for Barnabas, Paul might have remained in obscurity all of his life. We must try to imagine what the world would have missed had Paul not been discovered! Many people are waiting to be discovered for God.

Foreign Missions

Do we realize that we as Americans might have been pagans living in spiritual darkness and superstition were it not for the early Christian missionaries' travels to Europe? Thomas went to India; others went to Syria, Arabia and other countries. Shouldn't we as Americans believe in and strongly support missions?

Paul and Barnabas, the first foreign missionaries, traveled westward from Antioch (see Acts 13:1-4). The world's greatest enterprise is foreign missions, and this scene marked the start of this great movement. The whole idea began just the way all ideas should start—at a prayer meeting.

While Paul and Barnabas preached the gospel and suffered all kinds of persecution and hardship, many at home in Jerusalem were stirring up the most troublesome question the Church had ever faced: Must a Gentile become a Jew, accepting Jewish laws and ceremonies, in order to be saved (see 15:1)? Paul and Barnabas said nothing about the law of Moses; instead, they said, "Believe in the Lord Jesus, and you will be saved" (16:31). In other words, the Law itself doesn't save anyone.

Timothy joined the missionary party (see vv. 1-3). The first convert in Europe was not a famous scholar or some mighty ruler but a businesswoman, Lydia, "a dealer in purple cloth" (v. 14).

In Philippi, we find Paul and Silas in prison. Why do we find men like these locked behind iron bars (see vv. 16-24)? The second convert in Europe, the jailer, was very different from the first. Lydia converted during a prayer meeting, but it took an earthquake to convert the jailer. His question is one of the most important questions in all of history: "Sirs, what must I do to be saved?" (v. 30).

Paul's experiences in the greatest cities of his day are crowded with interest. He founded a church at Thessalonica (see 17:4). In Athens, Paul preached his immortal sermon on Mars Hill (see vv. 16-34). This is one of the greatest scenes in history. What effect did it have on those listeners (see v. 32)?

Paul not only spoke a wonderful message to the Athenians when he preached that day, but he also was speaking to us. Paul tells us that God is near. God hears our faintest whisper if we will only speak to Him.

"After this, Paul left Athens and went to Corinth" (18:1). We do not know whether he was successful in starting a church in Athens, but in Corinth, one of the most wicked cities of the ancient world, he founded a church and remained there 18 months to establish the people's faith (see vv. 8-11). Here Paul found Aquila and his wife, Priscilla, who became his loyal friends (see v. 18).

After an absence of three or four years, Paul returned to Antioch by way of Ephesus. In Antioch, he reported his entrance into Europe.

Paul's Third Missionary Tour

Next to Rome, Ephesus was perhaps the world's largest and most cosmopolitan city. Ephesus was notorious for its luxury, licentiousness and the worship of the goddess Artemis (referred to as "Diana of the Ephesians" in 19:28, *KJV*). Paul spent three years in Ephesus, preaching to multitudes of Jews and Gentiles of Asia. Enthusiastic converts burned their books on black arts and magic, and they threw away their silver idols. There was a great bonfire, which represented the converts' destruction of their old lives.

Paul teaches us that every idol must be torn down from its place in our hearts, and the Lord alone must occupy the throne. Is there anything in our lives that calls for a bonfire? Let's not be afraid of bringing ourselves face-to-face with anything that separates us from God.

Such blessings as this kind of enthusiasm without interference does not last long without opposition. If we read on to the end of Acts 19, we see the results of Paul's work. The silversmiths stirred up a riot, and the apostles were rescued from danger only by the help of the city officials.

As Paul traveled, he kept writing wonderful letters. We read them today with great profit and interest. From Ephesus, Paul sent his first Epistle to the Corinthians (see 1 Cor. 16:8). During this third journey, Paul wrote 2 Corinthians, Galatians and Romans.

Paul's Farewell

Paul's last missionary journey must have been a heartbreaking experience. He had to say good-bye at every place. He knew it was a final farewell. "They all wept as they embraced him and kissed him" (Acts 20:37), which is the Middle Eastern expression of sorrow—knowing they would never see him again. Probably no man, except David, has ever inspired such intense personal love in so many hearts.

Sailing out of the Ephesus harbor, Paul bid his friends a last farewell. He headed for Jerusalem, and from then on he is seen as "a prisoner for the Lord" (Eph. 4:1). Paul made his last visit to Jerusalem, where a swiftly formed mob gathered and rushed against the apostle and bound him, declaring he was teaching the Jewish people to forsake Moses. No doubt Paul recalled the fact that outside that city, he himself, 26 years before, had assisted in the murder of Stephen. However, finding out that Paul is a Roman citizen, the chief captain promised to give him a fair trial. Paul made his defense before the Roman governor, Felix at Caesarea (see 24:10-21). After two years of imprisonment, Paul was tried a second time before the new governor, Festus, and appealed from him to Caesar, the emperor (see 21:27—26).

Then Paul decided to set sail for Italy (see 27:1). After a

most exciting voyage, during which Paul's ship was wrecked in a terrific storm off the coast of Malta, Paul arrived in Rome. Here he was kept a prisoner in his own hired house for two years. Even though he was a prisoner, the great preacher and evangelist led Nero's servants to Christ (see 27—28:24). Service for God, the master, brightens even life's darkest hours. When we seek to lift others' burdens, we lighten our own.

During his imprisonment, Paul wrote many of his Epistles—Philemon, Colossians, Ephesians and Philippians. It was probably during a second imprisonment in a dungeon in Rome, expecting at any hour to be beheaded, that he wrote his second Epistle to Timothy.

Finally (according to tradition), the beloved apostle was condemned and beheaded. His heroic soul was released and his body was buried in the catacombs.

Paul changed the Early Church from a sect within Judaism to a worldwide influence. He worked to break down the barriers between Jew and Gentile and between slavery and freedom.

Acts is the only unfinished book in the Bible. It closes aburptly, but how else could it close? How could there be a complete account of a person's lifework as long as He lives? Our risen and ascended Lord still lives. From the center—Christ—the gospel message is still radiating in every direction, because "the uttermost part of the earth" (1:8, *KJV*) has not yet been reached. The gospel of Christ moves on! We are still living the Acts.

STUDY GUIDE

Henrietta Mears begins the chapter by stating: "Luke, in his Gospel, shows what Christ *began to do* on Earth; Acts shows what He *continued to do* by the Holy Sprit" (emphasis added).

1. Read Acts 1:1-5 closely, followed by Mears's summary of Luke's introduction. It is clear that she based "what Christ began to do on Earth" on verse one, but where does the idea that Jesus "continued to do [acts] by the Holy Spirit" come from?

2. Mears points out that the ascension of Jesus is the event that links the last scene in Luke and the first scene in Acts. Not many people, even in church, give much thought to the ascension of Christ as it relates to the right hand of the Father. How important is this teaching to you? Is it a throwaway doctrine or something that is as essential to you as the resurrection of Christ?

GOSPELS VERSUS ACTS

Traditionally, the full name of the book of Acts is "The Acts of the Apostles." However, notice that Henrietta Mears challenges the traditional title when she says: "Acts is not a record of the acts of the apostles; no extensive accounts are given of any of the apostles except Peter and Paul. Instead, Acts records the acts of the Holy Spirit through the apostles."

3. What does Mears think the proper title of the book should be? Why?

4. Do you prefer the traditional title or Mears's title?

We Are Called to Witness

Henrietta Mears continues her discussion by observing the importance of the word "witness" in Acts.

5. In a court of law, what does a witness do? What qualifications does a witness need to have?

6. The Greek word for "witness" originally looked like the word "martyr." Therefore, when many early Christians died witnessing for the gospel, the two words became closely associated. Which of Jesus' teachings emphasized the importance of witnessing to God's truth, even if threatened by death (see Matt. 10:38-39; Mark 8:34-38)?

7. How important is it to God and Christ that Christians faithfully witness to the gospel on Earth? Answer Mears's questions: "Are we witnessing for Christ? If not, why not?"

8. Henrietta Mears says Acts 1:8 is the heart of the book: "You will be my witnesses." There are many, many forms of witnessing for Christ. How many can you list?

Read Acts 8:26-39—the story of God's leading Philip to witness. God wants to use you to witness to others; He is preparing them to receive your witness. Not everyone will receive your witness immediately (and some won't want to hear it), but you can plant seeds that in time will ripen. If persistent, you will be used effectively by God.

9. Jesus says, "You will be my witnesses in Jerusalem, and in all Judea and Samaria, and to the ends of the earth" (Acts 1:8). This "widening circle of influence," as Mears calls it, accurately describes the outline of the entire book of Acts. Take a few minutes now to scan the whole book and see which chapters are devoted to Jerusalem, Judea and Samaria, and to the ends of the earth.

10. As you scan the chapters, keep a sharp eye out for what Mears calls "a marked outpouring of the Holy Spirit," as the gospel moves into new cultural areas. What do you find?

We Are Called to Missions

Henrietta Mears says, "No doubt Acts is the best guidebook to missions that has ever been written." But what is missions? Christian missions is the organized effort to bring the gospel of Christ to all the peoples on Earth—to plant viable, evangelizing churches in each of the planet's ethnic groups.

11. In our pluralistic culture, missions is seen as nothing but cultural imperialism. Read Acts 1:8 and Matthew

28:18-20. These are two versions of the same command—the Great Commission. According to these passages, who has given Christians authority to engage in missions? Do we have legitimate authority to bring the gospel to the ends of the earth? Who are we going to listen to—our culture or our Lord Jesus Christ?

12. If we have been given divine authority to engage in missions, who in the spiritual realm is against us? Do we have anything to fear from the spiritual forces who oppose Christian missions?

13. Christians understand that history is not just one event after another but that a greater story exists, which gives meaning to all human life. The pivotal point of this greater story was at the cross when Jesus Christ atoned for the sins of humanity. How can you personally get involved in this great historical project, which is the purpose of history?

14. In concluding this section, Mears mentions "the Early Church pursuing a definite program in carrying out its plans. Early Christians chose a great radiating center of population as a base from which the influence of their work might spread to the surrounding areas." Read Acts 13:1-2. What was the "great radiating center" in Acts?

Today there are many great cities that can be used as staging areas to reach the world. What great city is near you? How can you partner with others to reach the world with the gospel?

POWER FOR WITNESSING (ACTS 1—2)

Henrietta Mears opens this section exclaiming: "The disciples spent a wonderful 40 days with the Lord after His resurrection but before His ascension. How anxious they were to hear His last words of instruction!" And that's just what the disciples and believers in Christ learned—to hear God's instruction.

Wait on the Lord

In Acts 1:4-5, Jesus told the disciples to "wait." Wait? Hadn't they already spent three years with Jesus? Hadn't they already healed the sick and cast out demons? Hadn't Jesus already risen from the dead, demonstrating God's approval of His life and ministry?

15. Why do you think Jesus told the disciples to wait?

16. The disciples were supposed to "wait for the gift my Father promised, which you have heard me speak about" (Acts 1:4). Review John 13—17. What is Jesus talking about?

17. Jesus told the disciples to wait in Jerusalem. Mears observes that Jesus wanted them to stay in the great city of Jerusalem, even though they might have naturally wanted to leave because of the potential for persecution. She adds, "We cannot always choose our place of

service." Where is your Jerusalem right now? You might not have chosen it, but God has chosen you, for the time being, to be faithful where you are. How can you make the most of your situation for the sake of the gospel?

18. What role does the return of Christ—the Second Coming—play in our motivation to bring the gospel to all peoples?

Accept the Holy Spirit

19. Mears shares that the Holy Spirit came upon the believers and the Church was born. What is the absolute requirement for God's people to be effective and powerful witnesses for Christ?

What results follow when you are filled with the Holy Spirit, according to the Bible and to Henrietta Mears?

20. Mears observes that people made fun of the believers, thinking they were drunk (see Acts 2:13). We can never understand God or get close to God through unaided human reason. Why? What is the block? Do you agree with Mears that "rationalism never provides a reasonable explanation of anything divine"? Why or why not?

Walk with the Holy Spirit

Peter's sermon immediately follows the filling of the believers with the Holy Spirit—a great example of the earliest preaching of the Early Church. Mears states that Peter's challenge was to show his Jewish audience that Jesus, who had died an ignominious death on the Cross, was not cursed by God but was in fact God's anointed Messiah.

21. Read Deuteronomy 21:23. Why might Peter's Jewish audience have had reason to think that Peter was deceived about Jesus?

22. What arguments does Peter marshal to show that Jesus was in fact God's anointed Messiah?

Read Joel 2:28-32 and compare to Acts 2:15-21.

Read Acts 2:22. What did Jewish people pay particular attention to (see 1 Cor. 1:22)?

Read Acts 2:23. What is the appeal here?

Read Acts 2:24. What is the appeal here?

Read Psalm 16:8-11 and compare to Acts 2:25-28.

Read Acts 2:29-33. The argument was that if King David died, how could the promise about an eternal Kingdom apply to him (see 2 Sam. 7:13-14; Ps. 2). What do these verses in Acts say that could apply to this argument?

Read Psalm 110:1 and compare to Acts 2:34-36. King David never ascended to heaven to sit at God's right hand, but who did?

What do you think of Peter's sermon? Would it have been compelling to those gathered at the Feast of Pentecost?

23. Mears mentions several signs that prove the Church is a real church. What are they?

24. Are you seeing these signs in your church? If not, does anybody miss these signs not being present?

WITNESSING IN JERUSALEM (ACTS 3—8:3)

To start off this section, Mears opens with Peter's healing of an incurable cripple.

25. Read Matthew 10:1; Mark 3:14-15; Luke 9:1. Where did Peter get the idea that this was any way to witness?

26. What part does healing and driving out demons have in evangelism today? What indications are there in Scripture that these practices are to cease or were only for the Early Church?

27. What was the reaction of the religious leaders to healing and casting out demons? Why should Christians never be surprised when the gospel makes a breakthrough and opposition quickly comes?

28. What must the Church do when opposition occurs? Read the believers' full prayer in Acts 4:23-30. Did they

ask for relief from opposition or deliverance from persecution? What did they ask for? Note it carefully, and the next time you're catching static for the gospel, make these prayers your own.

29. Signs and wonders are not the whole enchilada. Mears points out that our lives need to fit in with the life of our risen Lord Jesus. You—and your life—are the only Bible most people will ever read. If people knew you well, would your life commend people to Christ or turn people off?

30. Despite the opposition, the Early Church continued to proclaim Christ (see Acts 5:42). Similarly, today there are Christians in India, Africa, China and the Muslim world who daily suffer shame for Christ's name. What can Western Christians do to show solidarity with their brothers and sisters in Christ in these countries that do not have religious freedom?

WITNESSING IN JUDEA AND SAMARIA (ACTS 8:4—12) AND WITNESSING IN EARTH'S UTTERMOST PARTS (ACTS 13—28)

In these two sections, the knottiest practical problem in the book of Acts, and probably the whole Bible, arises. In the Old Testament, Gentiles who wanted to align with God were expected to become Jewish, to reject their own ethnicity and to become part of the Jewish people. Mosaic Law and Jewish customs told

Gentiles exactly what they needed to do, including circumcision.

31. Given the life and teaching of Jesus and the opening of a New Covenant, had anything changed regarding the Gentiles who desired to align with God? If you had been a Jewish believer in Jesus who had followed the law of Moses from birth, the Law which you understood to have come directly from God, which way would you have answered? Why do you think the subject was so controversial?

32. Read the section of Mears's commentary on Saul and read Acts 9, particularly verse 15. It's easy to miss—with 2,000 years of Gentile Christian hindsight—but what premonition of big changes to come in the Jesus movement do you see in this verse?

33. Read the section of Mears's commentary on Peter and read Acts 10. In Acts 10:10-17, Peter—whom Jesus had designated the "rock," the leader of the apostles once Jesus passed from His earthly life (see Matt. 16:18-19)—had a very strange, thrice-repeated vision about all the unclean animals coming down on a sheet and being called "clean" by God. What do you think were Peter's first and second reactions to this vision?

34. As far as setting the stage for the problem, the clincher is Acts 10:44-48, in which Peter moved from a relatively noncommittal "I now realize how true it is that God does not show favoritism" (v. 34) to being willing

to baptize Gentiles (see vv. 47-48). What finally changed Peter's mind?

35. Eventually, the problem comes to a head in Acts 15, in which the Jerusalem Council—the heaviest hitters of the Early Church and all Jews themselves—arrived at a consensus decision (against almost everything they had been taught to believe beforehand) *not* to force the Gentiles to become followers of Moses' law in order to become full members of the Church. Read Galatians 1–2, in which Paul gives a brief history of his and Peter's ministry. How does Paul's recollection reflect the dynamics of the controversy?

36. The Jerusalem Council's decision was to enforce only one requirement—the Gentiles were not to disrespect the most sensitive of Jewish sensibilities (see Acts 15:29). How was this an amazingly open-minded decision? How was it a beautiful and wise compromise?

Seeing the Church in Transition

The Jerusalem Council's decision had far-reaching consequences for Western and world history. It opened the way for the Jesus movement to rapidly develop from a backwater Jewish sect into a new worldwide religion.

37. Read Genesis 12:3. Does the Jerusalem Council's decision fit in with God's promise to Abraham or seem to go against it?

38. Over time the Church gradually shifted from a Jewish-Hebrew emphasis to a Gentile-Greek dominance. Consider for a moment: What is your ethnic background? Do you know the history of how your ancestors first said yes to Jesus? Was it through missionaries? Traders? Or other means?

39. Unfortunately, the Gentile Church has not been as gracious to Jewish believers in Jesus as the Jewish Church was to Gentile believers in Acts 15. In the fourth century, Gentile church councils broke off friendly relations with Jews, including messianic Jews. Given the Christian persecutions, pogroms and holocausts against Jewish people in Western history, what do you think of these church council decisions?

40. One profound benefit coming out of Acts 15 is how the moral teachings of the Old Testament, like the Ten Commandments, penetrated and permeated Western culture and law. What evidence of this biblical influence can be found in America's founding documents?

41. Only since the 1960s has a genuinely Jewish movement of messianic synagogues sprung up. These synagogues are thoroughly Jewish, following Jewish customs, feasts, songs and liturgy—yet believing in Jesus! Shouldn't the Gentile Church fully accept messianic synagogues as full members of the Body of Christ? Do you know of any messianic synagogues worshiping

near you? Why not visit one sometime and show your appreciation and unity.

42. A continuing sticky question for Christian-Jewish relations concerns whether or not Gentile Christians should witness to Jewish people. Before you decide, don't just listen to the Jewish Defense League, but listen very closely to the messianic Jews! What do you think the messianic Jews' take on this question would be?

Living Life for God

Look at the last few verses of Acts 28. The account doesn't really have a conclusion; it's an ongoing story. It demands a sequel or many sequels! We are invited to live out the unwritten chapters of the book of Acts as we embrace the Holy Spirit and the values and goals this book wants to instill in the Church. Henrietta Mears recognized the need to continue the story: "The gospel of Christ moves on! We are still living the Acts."

43. "We must try to imagine what the world would have missed had Paul not been discovered! Many people are waiting to be discovered for God." One of the great things about Henrietta Mears is that she was always looking at the potential in people to make a difference for God. How can this attitude make you look at yourself differently? How about at others?

Get the Best-Selling Books
About the Best-Seller Ever

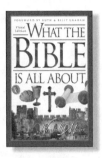

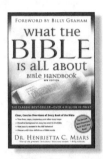

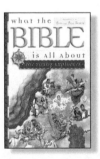
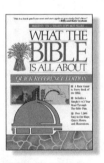